ICT and the Future of Health Insurance

George O. Obikoya

Table of Contents

Executive Summary

Health insurance is at the edge of a precipice. Profound changes around the industry are inevitably going to tip it over. The industry would have to move along with the other industries on which its very survival hinges. The health industry is one such significant influence on the health insurance industry. Progress in medical knowledge, and in information and other technologies, the ever-increasing healthcare costs, increasingly sophisticated public expectations of healthcare delivery, and emerging global health and economic issues are driving reforms in the health industry. These reforms are redirecting approaches to health service delivery and spurning new paradigms of health. That these new perspectives of health whose overall objective is to deliver comprehensive, qualitative, accessible and equitable healthcare, cost-effectively. There is increasing consensus that healthcare ICT diffusion is a crucial requirement for the realization of these goals. It is also critical for the insurance industry, and indeed, all healthcare stakeholders to appreciate fully, the interplay of the various drivers of contemporary health services delivery. This book explores in-depth these issues and how they work in tandem, and sometimes, even at variance but in the end to influence significantly the direction not just healthcare delivery, but associated industries, including the health insurance industry head.

Population health, disease prevention, health promotion, and the trend to community-based rather than hospital-based healthcare are gaining increasing currency in most developed countries regardless of whether they have private, or public health system or some mixture of the two. Considering that most healthcare spending is on hospitals and drugs, particularly prescription drugs, governments are understandably seeking ways to reduce these costs. Keeping the population healthy and treating them in ambulatory and domiciliary settings when they are ill are approaches that governments, particularly in developed countries with an aging population, hence high prevalence of chronic diseases that hitherto result in high hospitalization rates, now depend on to contain health spending. Many of these governments are therefore investing substantially on healthcare ICT, which not only provides the means to gather, store, communicate, and share patient data and information, all crucial to the effective operations of these new approaches to healthcare delivery, but also are important in improving the efficiency clinical and administrative processes.

While few would argue against the need for governments, to seek ways to reduce healthcare costs, the approaches to achieving, this goal varies among countries, and stir disputes within and between countries. This book also examines these controversies and their effects on healthcare finance. Healthcare ICT investments and health reforms in general. Would it not be counter-intuitive to expect that these developments would not influence the short-and long-term operations of the health insurance industry? What does the industry need to know and do in order to fit in seamlessly into this new dispensation in the health industry? What should be the nature and extent of the collaboration between the health and insurance industries for each to achieve its strategic objectives? What does the future portend for the health insurance industry considering the developments in the healthcare industry? How would the outcomes of these developments and those of the collaboration or otherwise between the health and insurance industries affect the future of both industries? The answers to these questions, which this book attempts to provide, would reveal the subtle dynamics that underlie the tenuous relationship between these two industries and what both need to do not just to strengthen it both to ensure its continuity and their own very survival.

Health is increasingly a major strategic resource. Technological progress permeates all aspects of modern life. Not just the public but also governments are expecting technology to help deliver better health services. There is no doubt that these expectations are reasonable, but equally none that they would require significant investments in healthcare ICT research and development, and in implementation and its widespread diffusion in the healthcare delivery for their actualization. Does the insurance industry also need to invest in healthcare ICT, and to what extent if so? What would be the return on its investment, and would this return be short-or long-term, or both? The insurance industry would need to find answers to such questions now, in order to develop a realistic healthcare ICT strategy that is in consonance with its own vision of its future. This book also discusses the role information technology would play in enhancing the capabilities of the health insurance industry to benefit from its collaboration with the health industry in ensuring that it has the necessary data and information, required in decision making on vital insurance operations such as pricing, and billing, among others.

Introduction

T he oil crisis and recession got most of the blame for the increasing costs of healthcare in most of countries of the Western world in the 1970s through the 1990s. These increases were as much as 36% and 26% of the GDP (Gross Domestic Product, or the total value of goods and services a country produces) in the US and the UK respectively between 1972 and 1982, and 36% and 20% between 1982 and 1992. However, it is doubtful that healthcare costs would have dropped even if recession did not slow GDP growth considering the increasing healthcare needs of the aging population of these countries. Government foots most of the healthcare bills in many EU countries, in Canada, and indeed in most OECD (Organization of Economic Cooperation and Development) countries, and even in the US, about 45% of the bills. Healthcare reforms are also recurrent activities in these countries, often triggered by concerns about increasing healthcare costs, mediocre public health outcomes, public sector deficits, and some would argue, the invisible hand of the prevailing view of the zeitgeist on what role government should play in our affairs. T here are of course many other reasons governments embark on healthcare reform, but most of them revolve around healthcare costs, with doctors, some assert, the chief cost drivers. Questions are beginning to arise regarding the central role physicians play in the allocation of health resources, particularly with regard to their choices of services to patients, including hospitalizations, medications prescribed, lab tests ordered, and so on, and the cost implications of these decisions, including for the health insurance industry. Indeed, the call for accountability and more efficient and cost-effective resource allocation continues to boom louder, resulting in some countries, new legislation to ensure compliance. The public is also interested in the unfolding saga. There is increasing demand for higher quality health services, patient safety, privacy, confidentiality, and security of patient information, and quicker access to care. These are also reasons governments are initiating healthcare reforms, which incidentally are emerging in various models, including managed care, managed competition reform, internal market reform, and a host of others. To be sure, these various models have their merits and flaws. However, they also have a common denominator, which is to provide better, less expensive, cost-effective, and more sustainable health services. Some would insist physicians do not like outsiders, for example, governments and insurers, prying into their professional affairs. Indeed, there should be no dispute about physicians prerogative on therapeutic modalities, but also precious little about providers of funds used to run health services having the right to demand cost-effective use of the funds. It may sound like a somewhat treacherous path to trod trying to find a meeting point between the interests of physicians, providers of healthcare funds, and the public, but it is not nearly that impossible a goal to achieve. It only takes a commitment on all sides to work towards the goal. Physicians need to start their own "internal" reform, which essentially is to seek ways to make the services that they recommend and provide more cost-effective, and yet meet the needs of the patients they serve. This would require a positive change in attitude toward healthcare ICT. How many physicians for example would doubt the value of evidence-based practice in rational care provision and in resource allocation and optimization? From EMR (electronic medical record) to CPOE (computerized physician order entry), to RFID (Radio Frequency Identification), and to many of the variety of DSS (decision support systems) available on the market, there is no shortage of health ICT solutions that can enable physicians provide better quality and more cost-effective services. Physicians only need to embrace and adopt these technologies, but should governments and insurers, not want to facilitate this healthcare ICT diffusion in the form of incentives and even financial support? The public also needs reassurance, including that effective IT security are in place, regarding the safety and security of their personal information in order for them to feel more comfortable about electronic health/ medical records and to be more willing to participate in their use. Does the interest of the public in healthcare ICT not matter were insurers to exploit fullest the benefits of their healthcare ICT investments? Telehealth is making health services more accessible to persons living in remote and underserved areas, and electronic health record (EHR) is reducing healthcare costs and improving the quality of care by making crucial patient information available to physicians and other healthcare professionals in real time at the point of care (POC.) There is a lot more healthcare ICT is doing and can do to make the provision of qualitative, accessible, equitable, and sustainable health services what it should be in the new millennium. However, there is no gainsaying the need for concerted effort for these objectives to materialize.

Health Key-Player Dynamics and ICT Diffusion

Purchasers, insurers, providers, and suppliers are the key players on the healthcare scene. Purchasers and insurers are both payers, the former providing the funds to the latter, which then pays providers, such as doctors and other healthcare professionals. Individuals paying even in part for their health services are also payers. Suppliers are the drug, medical equipments, and ICT companies that supply providers. Payers incur expenses for every cent spent on health, suppliers, and providers, on the other hand accrue revenue, which creates an enduring conflict of interest on containing health costs between the two groups. With hospitals and drug firms feuding over prices, doctors over capitation payments, and insurers scheming to trim physician reimbursement yet requesting more purchaser funds, there can be no understating the significance of the unending interplay of these opposing interests on healthcare expenditures and dynamics. Governments are in general payers, purchasers, and insurers of healthcare in many countries including Canada and the U.S. With government health spending increasing exponentially in recent times, the call for cost-containment is becoming louder. The U.S. spends more on health than any other country. In 2002, the country spent $5267 per person on health care, compared to Switzerland s $3445, which came next in health spending, and to those of Norway, Canada, and Germany, in decreasing order of health spending, which were less than 60% that of the U.S. and even lesser, that of the U.K, $2160 per capita, just 41% of U.S. health spending. U.S. health spending rose by 7.7% in 2003, with annual growth projections of 7.2% between now and 2013, by which time the country s health expenditures would be approximately $3.6 trillion or 18.4% of its gross domestic product (GDP.) Canada plans to spend $41 billion on its health system over the next decade, with an additional $805 million over the next five fiscal years. The 2005 health budget of the U.K is £ 90bn, for both countries significant increases over previous years. Australia now spends twice as much as it did in 1996 on health and aged care, and plans to spend $45 billion in 200/06, an increase of $20 billion since 1996.

Increasing health expenditures are typical, rather than exceptional in many other developed countries. Many of these countries, particularly in Europe have quasi-socialist governments in power, with a mandate to improve their citizens wellbeing. They are therefore obliged to provide their peoples with qualitative health services, or risk their wrath at the next elections. Yet, even these governments cannot afford continuing rise in health expenditures in the long term given, let us assume, that they could in the short term. Indeed, even in the U.S., the richest country in the world, containing health spending has become almost a mantra. However, this may not be easy to achieve considering the dynamics amongst the healthcare key players, with health purchasers and insurers in general aspiring to trim health spending, providers and suppliers, for more of it. There are many reasons for rising health costs, many contentious, but that hospital care and drug expenses feature prominently among them is immutable. In 2002, heart diseases, cancer, trauma, psychiatric disorders, and lung diseases were the five most costly chronic and acute diseases in the U.S., with expenditures highest for cancer ($4500/ year), although it was the least prevalent, and lung diseases, the most prevalent. Many developed countries have similar disease prevalence and patterns. Perhaps even more significantly, many of these diseases have preventable risk factors, and with stronger emphasis on public health programs, could become less prevalent, with significant savings in healthcare costs. Coupled with free health market wherein health insurance plans contracted to hospitals at low costs although not with insurers raising premiums whimsically or seeking more funds from government while cutting provider reimbursement; and cost sharing principles, which do not price the poor out or force excessive government and insurer intervention, this emphasis on public health will likely contain health spending. Indeed, attention to service delivery approaches in general needs to move beyond academic pedantry over which of mass campaigns or general health services is more cost-effective for disease control. Could any Western government deny the economic burden of chronic, non-communicable diseases, such as Diabetes? Is the public not concerned about these diseases and their consequences? Do we not have the technical tools to tackle them, the health services infrastructure to follow-up the campaign phase, or is it logistically and administratively infeasible? What then is unwise about launching a mass campaign against such diseases if we answered in the affirmative to these questions? How much could we save on health spending in the long term embarking on such mass campaigns, or even if general health services focused on a limited set of prioritized, cost-effective interventions, rather than what some regard as the selectivity of mass campaigns?

The other two key players on the health scene, the providers and suppliers, are perhaps the most problematic regarding healthcare cost-containment vis-à-vis its dynamics. There are intra-and inter-group conflicts operating in these groups and between them and the healthcare payers that are not only important for health costs, but that are key drivers of health economy, chief of which is the tussle between resisting and seeking health spending. The direction these conflicts go at any point in time varies with a country's economic prosperity, prevailing health policy and reform process, government regulations of health insurance, health outcomes indicators, availability, distribution, and remuneration of physicians, new drug development, and medical and technological progress among many others. It is not per chance that technological progress stands out among these factors. Its role in the evolution of our civilization is sterling. In particular, ICT has become an essential part of modern healthcare delivery, driving not only its progress, but also reducing its costs over the long term. Indeed, recent developments in the health industry underscore the recognition it is receiving from all the industry's four key players. From 1997 to 2003, the Canadian government invested about $1.5 billion in a variety of health-related ICT projects, funded through different federal organizations and entities, including Health Canada, Human Resource Development Canada, Industry Canada, National Defense, Veterans Affairs, and CANARIE Inc. The government spent $126 million in 2004 on health ICT through Canada Health Infoway, and plans to spend $195 million, 56% more than last year. European countries health ICT spending in 2004 was 14 billion Euros, an amount expected to double in 2005. Many other developed countries are also spending more on health ICT.

The U.S. government awarded three contracts totaling $17.5 million to encourage widespread adoption of information technology in healthcare on October 07, 2005. The U.S. National Coordinator for Health Information, Dr David Brailer, noted that the contracts followed the federal government s call for proposals earlier this year to develop a certification protocol for healthcare IT tools; synchronize health information standards; deal with differences in privacy and security laws in business policies and states; and test prototypes for a national health information network. The day before the announcement of the contracts, the Agency for Healthcare Research and Quality (AHRQ) of the Department of Health and Human Services (HHS) announced the award of over $22.3 million to 16 grantees to implement health information technology (Health IT) systems to improve the safety and quality of health care. HHS also announced two proposed rules to eliminate the legal hindrances to healthcare providers sharing IT with physicians, an attempt by HHS to speed up the adoption of electronic prescribing tools and electronic health records (EHR.) On October 05, 2005, U.S. health officials proposed new rules that will exempt high-tech gifts from federal laws limiting the goods doctors can receive gratis from health-care providers. These new regulations will make it easier for doctors, particularly in solo or small practices, to receive free software, computers, and allied services for EHR, and shield physicians and health care firms, from litigation were hospitals, pharmacy benefits managers, IT vendors, and others to pay to install electronic medical record systems in physicians offices. Indeed, many legislators have submitted bills to the U.S. Congress to provide incentives also in order to facilitate ICT adoption.

HHS officials contend that adopting ICT is not only important in reducing healthcare costs, but also in monitoring side effects, and eliminating mistakes, particularly in drugs prescribing, critical issues to address in light of the 1999 Institute of Medicine (IOM) report that 44,000 to 98,000 U.S. patients died annually from medical errors. Further, a recent RAND study revealed that improved efficiency could save the U.S. some $77 billion. Expected to follow soon, and to streamline practice further saving costs are regulations detailing electronic prescription rules for firms participating in the new Medicare prescription drug plan. Insurers are also keen on ICT adoption, their position, and opportunities for profitability enhanced by such government regulations as the Health Insurance Portability and Accountability Act (HIPAA), which among others stipulate standards for protecting patient privacy and information security. Yet, only 14% of all American medical groups use EHR, according to a recent study the US Medical Group Management Association in Colorado initiated. According to this survey of over 3,000 group practices, only 11.5% had fully implemented EHR, 12.5% with five or less full-time-equivalent physicians had, 15% for groups with 6 to 10 physicians, 19%

for those with 11 to 20, and 19.5% for those with 20 or more doctors. The RAND study also found similar figures with about 15 to 20 percent of doctors' offices and about 20 to 25 percent of hospitals having an EHR implemented. These figures bring why governments are instituting measures, for example providing doctors with over $7,000 each in Alberta, Canada, to facilitate EHR adoption in particular, and health ICT diffusion in general, sharply into focus.

It is logical to assume that because the financial interests of health providers and suppliers are diametrically opposed to those of purchasers and insurers, doctors, ICT vendors, pharmaceutical companies and others in these two latter key categories pose a challenge to the efforts of the former two, particularly of government, to contain health costs. To be sure, the role of insurers (other than government) in trimming health costs is somewhat contentious, except perhaps in a situation where government-regulated managed competition prevents health plans from deliberately and selectively enrolling healthy people, as occurred in the Medicare HMO program in the U.S. not long ago. Further, administrative costs of private health insurance in the U.S has risen up to 16% annually between 2003 and 2005. The costs of prescription drugs in the U.S increased at 11% in the past three years, and hospital and physician expenditures grew annually during the same period at 7-8%. Canada spent $15 billion on prescription and non-prescription drugs in 2001, $12.3% on just the former 10.6% more than it did in 2000. Its drug expenditures for 2004 were $21.4 billion in 2004, 8.8 percent more than the previous year, and five times more than it spent in 1985, prescription drugs walloping $18-billion, up 10.2 per cent from 2003. A rise in the number of prescriptions doctors write, in the prices of drugs, and the use of more expensive drugs, which latter some blame on the so-called aggressive direct-to-customer (DTC) marketing strategy of pharmaceutical firms are some of the reasons studies found account for the increasing costs of prescription drugs. The reasons notwithstanding, purchasers, including patients, bear the brunt, which explains why many Americans, including seniors have been crossing the border to buy drugs in Canada, even if Canadians themselves pay some of their prescription drug bills, albeit for some, via the private insurance coverage their employers provide, and for others, meaning they cannot afford some medications they badly need.

Some argue that government tries to contain prescription drugs costs by delaying the approval process of new drugs, a process further complicated in Canada because each province has a review committee for approving drugs for its formulary; and that streamlining this process would speed approval for life-saving drugs that could reduce hospital stay, saving costs on long-term care. Some even contend that by reducing "time-to-market" for these drugs, it would also reduce the prices of drugs. Meantime, the battle for market share between the generic and brand forms of medications is becoming tougher. These various cost-reducing factors face-off against the resolve of pharmaceutical companies to recoup the time and money invested in research and development, and drug production and marketing. Right in the midst of all these epic battles are doctors, after all, they prescribe these medications, and decide which ones to prescribe, how many, and in what quantities. Doctors determine which lab tests or ancillary investigations to carry for diagnostic and evaluative purposes. They also decide which patient to hospitalize and for how long, the surgical procedure a patient needs, and whether it should be immediate or elective. There is no doubt that doctors, play a significant role in the dynamics of healthcare and that they have the potential to drive down health costs. The question is whether they are really helping to reduce healthcare costs. It may not seem so looking at the statistics cursorily but they are also unlikely to want health costs to rise on purpose. Being in the interest of society for healthcare delivery to be safe, qualitative, yet cost-effective, it is incumbent on doctors to embrace appropriate "system-based" interventions to achieve these goals.

One such intervention is the use of ICT in healthcare delivery. From EHR, to electronic prescribing, to computerized physician order entry (CPOE), and radio frequency identification (RFID), to improving the hospital design and workflow using IT and robotics, advances in health ICT have proven effective for reducing medical errors, improving patient safety, facilitating information sharing and delivery at the point of care (POC), reducing hospitalization rates, and improving quality of care. Computerized evidence-based practice ensures rational prescribing and optimization of scarce resources. Developments in artificial intelligence (AI) are making surgeons able to operate without being physically present. Nanotechnology and genomics promise "smart-drugs" and the possible eradication of certain diseases. The Rehabilitation Institute of Chicago is fitting the disabled with computerized (bionic) arms, which function just like normal arms. A computer chip implanted on the retina is helping individuals with retinal blindness to see once again. Doctors at the Functional Electrical Stimulation Center in Cleveland are placing implants in the chest walls of patients paralyzed from the neck downwards (quadriplegia), connected to a complex array of computer chips and electrodes, which enable them move their upper limbs to function normally, with the hope that the lower limbs would be able to function likewise in future. The list of ICT-related revolutionary treatments is becoming even longer as governments and biotechnology firms, among others, continue to invest substantially in research activities worldwide. So, does anyone need cajole doctors to embrace ICT? While it is arguable that healthcare delivery is even played out on the world stage these days, doctors still have immense responsibilities to ensure the health system works, at least within the confines of their country. They will unlikely inspire other members of the clinical team that they lead to see the central role of ICT in healthcare delivery, or be helping in the efforts to trim health costs, shunning ICT for whatever reasons.

ICT and Public Health

 P ublic health is a critical aspect of any health system. Many of the factors that determine health or ill health are controllable by appropriate public health measures. It is therefore, possible to improve the health of the citizenry by instituting effective public health programs, and by strengthening the capacity of and improving the efficiency of public health systems. It is likewise possible to prevent diseases through public health education and campaigns, among other measures. Indeed, healthcare systems worldwide face increasing pressure to develop health policy and program initiatives that reallocate more institutional resources to community-based programming, develop novel, cost-effective healthcare delivery, and promote coordination and integration of health services at local, provincial, state, and federal levels. Yet, most countries' health dollars still fund hospital services and prescription drugs and in the U.S. administrative costs of private health insurance as well. Health costs have been rising steadily in many developed countries in recent times. It is unlikely anyone would complain though who believes that increased health spending improves health outcomes by facilitating access to new technologies and treatment modalities, that it creates employment opportunities and increases income, or that it is unlikely to affect other economic sectors in a growing economy adversely. On the other hand, such increased spending would likely aggravate the company executive who has to buy high premium employee health insurance. Nor is a Treasury Secretary likely to be blissful who has to struggle with budget deficits or to look for resources for other services besides health, or to agonize over eligibility deductions with the prospects of many poor, elderly, and infirmed losing Medicaid benefits. Would it then be moot that increased healthcare spending may in fact lead to decreased access to care? Regardless of whether one sees increased healthcare spending as constituting a strain on or driving economic development, the debate on rising healthcare costs has filtered out of its usual academic, business, and government confines, and now features in the everyday lexicon of non-experts alike.

U.S. federal government estimates indicate that the country's health expenditures would increase from $1.6 trillion in 2002 or 14.9% of its Gross Domestic Product (GDP), a

14

measure of the value of all goods and services it produces, to $3.6 trillion in 2013, or 18.4% of GDP. Some would query the wisdom in measuring health expenditures as percentages of GDP, for example because GDP growth varies from one year to the next, which if rapidly increasing, as it did in the US in the 1990s, may falsely suggest that health spending is static, or that it is too high, as in the subsequent economic slump. Further, how staggering is a 3.5% increase in health spending over eleven years, considering developments in our world today? Let us even for now disregard the distinction between costs and expenditures, often used synonymously, but which considering the production process implied in the former would make why health spending based on the latter, the funds used to buy goods and services is much lesser, immediately obvious. Perhaps we should also note the intricacy of using private health insurance premiums as the barometer for health spending, since not only may increasing premiums not tally with rising health expenditure since the latter may rise slower than the former, but also because health insurers may raise premiums to compensate for outstanding losses.

No matter how we measure health spending, the fact that it is rising is not deniable, nor is any suggestion that it will likely continue to do so, implausible. The reasons for this rising costs are legion, and range from high administrative costs, to inadequate or lack of free market, to costs of technologies, of prescription drugs, to lack of cost-containment and poor governance. There is no shortage of ideas on why health spending is rising, although this may not be true for how to curb it, or rather, which solutions have worked-public, private, or hybrid health system, regardless. Should we therefore brace up for the inevitable, that health expenditures will continue to increase? Alternatively, should we discountenance technological progress in order to cut health spending, for example, or a new treatment modality capable of saving the lives of millions or attenuating their pain? If we did, should we ask how much buffer does even the most bountiful economy have to withstand the onslaught of a catastrophic pandemic for example? Our world has changed so much that we need new economic paradigms to manage its increasing complexity, including the conundrum of exorbitant health spending in our new age.

That an appropriate starting point in solving this problem is the direction that public health is going does not diminish the significance of hospital, ambulatory care, or other types of healthcare. However, it underscores the next frontier of health economics. In other words, any country seriously contemplating curtailing health spending needs a closer look at its public health policies and programs. While it may sound Utopian, the ultimate goal of public health is to prevent diseases and promote physical, mental, and emotional wellbeing, through activities such as infectious disease surveillance and control, disease prevention with vaccination programs for example, health campaigns to promote wellness and healthy living, and population health analyses, among others. What makes public health so important? The answer is not that obscure. Consider the US for example. As with other developed countries, it spends more per capita on health than countries not so endowed, but also far more than those comparably wealthy, with only slight differences in their GDP per capita, which clearly suggests that there is more involved in health spending than GDP per capita. Is it the country's aging population, after all, it is reasonable to expect that per capita health expenditures on the elderly would surpass those on younger people? However, research evidence refutes this assumption, which in fact explains less than 10% of health spending growth, some studies finding no correlation between population aging and health spending. Rather, per capita health expenditures on the elderly are rising, slower than on younger persons, because the percentage of the population that is elderly is increasing comparatively slowly. Coupled with decreasing disability years, controlling for several disease risk factors in the elderly, the increasing high prevalence of obesity, diabetes, and the metabolic syndrome, increasing health costs correlates stronger with the young than the elderly.

Many diseases and health problems of young persons and persons under 65 years are preventable, including their short-and long-term consequences. Many of these conditions are life-style related, and even those with genetic diathesis often manifest in combination with environment triggers. A variety of microbial, including bacterial, viral, and parasitic infections are increasingly responsible for substantial health burden worldwide, many borne by the water we drink, our food, mosquitoes, flies, and our other seemingly benign cohabitants of the planet. Some of these health problems have always existed, but newer "smart" bugs are mutating into deadly genomic profiles. Investing more in public health measures is now no longer an option, it is imperative, lest we throw up our arms in capitulation to enemies we sometimes need electron microscopes to see. Where in any case are we going to find the resources to clean up the mess, after say an avian flu pandemic has succeed in causing 150 million deaths, and possibly thrice more acutely ill or dying? Yet, how many countries are confident about their preparedness for such a pandemic. With the virus having made its way from birds into humans, how much longer would it take it to mutate into a form capable of human-to-human transmission, and via the jumbo jet crisscross the globe?

It is possible to prevent this chilling scenario by instituting appropriate pubic health reforms, and establishing necessary public health programs, for example, developing and storing sufficient quantities of anti-bird flu vaccine. Would it not be more cost-effective than not preparing adequately for what experts regard as imminent? Avian flu is now afflicting people and causing deaths in Turkey, Europe s east fringe, droplets of birds migrating from the Far East, its harbinger. It seems just a matter of time before it spreads throughout the continent and across the Atlantic. Implementing appropriate public health services will also help prevent other diseases and minimize their burden on society, including eventually reducing health spending. Informing, educating, and empowering the people; health status monitoring; developing health policies and plans; connecting people to the health services they need; evaluating services; disease surveillance; bioterrorism monitoring; and population health analysis, are some of such public health services. ICT not only facilitates these services, conducting many without ICT creates profound logistics problems, often with significant cost implications. Need we wait for the inevitable increase in health expenditures rather than invest now in public health, and in ICT, its essential enabler? ICT, deployed at all health services levels and tailored to their particular needs, and that communicate in tandem for the effective operations of public health activities will not only facilitate disaster preparedness, but also the subsequent relief efforts in the event of a disaster, saving enormous costs in human and material terms.

Some would argue for other measures they deem more effective in reducing healthcare costs, for example, a free health market governed by the laws of supply and demand, which would in theory foster competition and increase patient cost sharing. However, because of disparity in the availability and accessibility of health services, the poor lacking the resources to compete effectively, and insurance coverage obviating the need to seek lowest cost services, among other reasons, the competitiveness of such a free market is questionable, although not when health insurance plans shop for hospitals with the best yet most cost-effective services. Furthermore, the RAND Health Insurance Experiments of the 1970s clearly showed that participants that had free health services utilized them more than participants that paid part of the cost did. There is therefore, some merit in a free health market arrangement, but to argue that there is also merit in strengthening public health is beyond reproach, not to mention the chaos that would envelope the secondary healthcare system in the wake of a disaster, natural or manmade that doing so might have prevented.

ICT and Health Insurance

Health insurance, a form of insurance, which could be public or private, whereby the insurer pays the costs of health services that the insured received when ill due to covered causes, or accidents, continues to stir controversy particularly , private health insurance in developed countries. The reasons for this hullabaloo are legion. Public health insurance has its critics, and of course, proponents, equally passionate about their respective viewpoints as are those in opposing camps on private health insurance, each camp, ready with its lists of the merits of its cause, and the woes of the other s. Some countries such as Canada have publicly funded health systems, albeit with a tinge of private funding. Others such as the Unites States have a predominantly private health insurance system. Yet others, such as the United Kingdom, Australia and New Zealand and many European countries have varying combinations of both. None of these countries or their health systems could claim to provide its citizens with flawless health services. On the other hand, health systems, private, or public, or somewhere in between, labor under intense strain, in these countries for a variety of reasons of both internal and external origins, many undergoing reforms in order to solve the multiplicity of problems that often confront them. Meantime, those who need the health services bear the brunt, which at times could put people s lives in jeopardy. Consider the hypothetical case of Lucy. Diagnosed with kidney failure, she was on periodic dialysis for years. Prior to her husband s death, his private health insurance paid for Lucy s treatment, but not anymore. Forced to take one, she struggled to pay her $200 monthly premium for years, but she no longer can afford its current $4500 monthly coverage costs. Left with no option, Lucy dropped out of the insurance plan, and now quietly awaits her imminent demise. Lucy may be fictitious, but this is the experience of many people in some countries for example the US, which rely mainly on private health insurance. Indeed, an estimated 45.8 million people were without medical coverage in 2004, an increase of 859,000 people from 2003, according to a report released August 30, 2005, by the U.S. Census Bureau, which reports the number of uninsured Americans as those without health insurance for the entire year. What is more, hospitals routinely charge uninsured people up to four times as much than insured patients, the US House

Energy, and Commerce subcommittee on oversight and investigations, heard from financial experts on June 23, 2005, debt collectors hounding these monetarily challenged individuals, to crown it all1. In 2002, hospitals in the Philadelphia area, for example, charged an average of $30,000 to treat a heart attack, most insurers ultimately paying less than $10,000. Analysts explain the reason for this over billing, sometimes thrice, even four times what managed care, or government programs pay, being hospitals efforts to recoup increasing costs of indigent care. It does not seem to help the uninsured, for example, that every hospital under Ascension Health, one of the largest nonprofit Catholic hospital systems, lost money in 2004, on the services they gave the uninsured. Nor does it that even if these hospitals, and many like them, wanted to help the indigent, offering discount programs or allowing patients to negotiate their bills, for examples, they stood the chance of running foul of federal fraud laws.

A 2004 study that Families USA, a Washington-based national advocacy group commissioned showed that about 82 million people, roughly a third of the U.S. population younger than 65 years did not have health insurance at some point in the previous two years. Most of who in fact had lacked it for over nine months2. The study also found that middle-class Americans are also part of the uninsured population, the increase in the number of uninsured blamed on rising health care costs, a soft labor market with employers relinquishing more health costs to workers and reductions in state safety net programs, among others. The percentage of the uninsured was around 15.7 percent in both 2003 and 2004, the actual number of insured persons rose by 2 million, to 245.3 million (84.3 percent of the population), between 2003 and 2004, although the rise in the number of those uninsured, from 45 million in 2003 to 45.8 million in 2004, offset these figures. The percentage of people with employer-based health insurance also fell from 60.4 percent in 2003, to 59.8 percent in 2004. In 2003, 34% of American firms did not offer their workers health insurance, and in the firms that did workers could not afford the share of the premiums the firms asked them to contribute. Furthermore, workers in between jobs often cannot pay the cost of COBRA or other health insurance for that matter. The Consolidated Omnibus Budget Reconciliation Act (COBRA) continuation coverage, which provides certain former employees, retirees, and their dependants the right to temporary continuation of health coverage at group rates, has its setbacks. Not only is the coverage only available under certain conditions, group health coverage for COBRA participants, is usually more expensive than for active employees. This is because the employer pays a part of the premium for active employees but COBRA participants pay all of it themselves. Furthermore, as many as 14 million low-income workers do not benefit from the safety net of the public programs meant to provide health coverage for 56 million Americans due to the complicated array of exclusion criteria. Indeed, recent events in the US highlight some of these problems and stress the need for some form government intervention. The aftershocks of Hurricane Katrina have spilled over into private health insurance. According to the Chicago Tribune of December 29, 2005, Blue Cross and Blue Shield of Louisiana estimated that as many as 200,000 Louisiana residents would lose their employee-sponsored health insurance as companies struggle with finances and lay-off staff, and some even fold up. Government did in fact intervene in this instance, but a state requirement that insurance companies keep medical policies active even in cases of unpaid premiums expired in November 2005, with insurance firms now poised to nullify such insurance policies. Insurers are also feeling the effects of Hurricane Katrina with the increasing numbers of "health insurance whipping", whereby displaced workers take on and lose temporary jobs, some with, others without health insurance. There is also the pressure on the health system, whose infrastructure and staff severely depleted, are reluctant to add the burden of treating the uninsured to their plateful of problems. These problems underscore the need for changes in health insurance policies at state and federal levels to address issues of coverage for workers better than COBRA and similar legislation do, currently. Some have suggested universal healthcare coverage as the solution to the gaping chasms in health insurance coverage, and Illinois for example, seems to have heard, and is responding to this call. In 2005, the state became the first in the US to offer comprehensive health insurance coverage to all children via its "All Kids", health coverage proposal, which Governor Blagojevich, State Senate President Emil Jones, and House Speaker Michael J Madigan, put forward[3]. The plan would certainly help the 253,000 uninsured children in the state whose parents could not afford to buy them insurance coverage, but according to the Census Bureau figures for 2004, 18.9 percent of children in poverty, and 11.2 percent of children overall in the country did not have health insurance. Would other states follow suit, at least so that children have universal health insurance coverage in the country? Should every

American not actually have health insurance cover, some would ask, health being a basic human right? May be the question should be why this is not the case? Some think the answer is simple, that US policy makers just need to accept the fact that they have reached the zenith of the maneuverability of the health system, which started post WWII, since when they have expanded both public and private insurance coverage, simultaneously struggling with the cost penalties of the demand the resulting insurance-financing mechanisms engendered. This argument ends up asserting that it is no longer possible to expand health insurance, which leaves public and private plan sponsors no option but to start to reduce the coverage they offer, and policymakers concerned about accessibility to care and equity, to become innovative, adopting for example, strategies that foster direct service delivery4. Indeed, there is a multiplicity of viewpoints regarding the answer to America's health insurance woes, but no one would likely disagree that there is need for innovation in service delivery models, or that underlying this innovation is the implementation of appropriate healthcare ICT. There is little doubt that health insurance would have to operate in tandem with technology deployment in the conduct of their business and in healthcare delivery for any significant changes to occur in the various parameters relevant to healthcare costs, and those that convey the pervasiveness of a comprehensive healthcare package to the entire citizenry. There are important questions regarding why they would, though particularly considering that their objectives do not necessarily coincide with those of government in a privately funded healthcare insurance milieu such as the United States. Here again, some might consider the answer quite simple: government makes them do so or, that they have social responsibility or that profit motive does not preclude compliance with contractual agreements with consumers, or some such coercion-based answer. True as they may be, the realities are not necessarily that simple. Unlike public health insurance, private insurance firms are business ventures, answerable to their shareholders and management boards. Their mandate is to return profits and not philanthropy. Yet, their charge is to provide healthcare for non-corporate clients, ordinary people who know nothing about the goings-on inside the boardrooms but simply need medical attention when they or their family members fall ill. This is just one instance of the conflicts private insurance firms confront that are at the core of the criticisms levied against the industry and why some are adamant that private health insurance is fundamentally flawed. Let us examine these conflicts, which are not country-specific in a bit more detail.

Health insurers whether public or private underwrite risks, some high others low. Both need to survive to do so. Government sponsor of publicly funded health insurance in countries such as Canada would unlikely be able to accommodate ever-increasing healthcare costs indefinitely, private health insurance, even more unlikely to do so. Government for example would likely offset the increasing costs due to increased health service usage when out-of-pocket medical costs fall due to subsidies, with increased taxes, private insurance by raising premiums, termed ex-post moral hazard. Public health insurance covers all risks, but private ones, tend to avoid high-risk clients, for examples, the elderly who are likely to suffer from chronic illnesses, those individuals that engage in unhealthy, risky behaviors, such as smokers, and heavy drinkers. Indeed, unlike public insurance, which covers everyone, private insurance firms also face the issue of "adverse selection", that is the tendency of people with imminent or current health problems to enroll, or engage in risky behaviors once enrolled, termed ex-ante moral hazard. Insurance companies argue that providing health coverage for high-risk clients is expensive and could mean raising premiums, which could affect low-risk clients if not price them out ultimately, one reason some people in the US and other countries that rely on private insurance lack coverage. This is one reason why some advocate risk equalization, which is currently causing mêlée in Ireland. This is a compensation system in the health insurance sector, under which health insurers, which have relatively younger members, would have to make payments to competitors, which have a relatively older subscriber base. It is also an example of the conflict of interest that critics of private health insurance would readily mention, given these insurers' responsibility to provide healthcare coverage, or is it? Private insurance providers would likely argue that they are responsible for honoring their contractual obligations to their enrollees and nothing more. It is another matter at what price they provide the services, and if this prices some people out, in response to which they would likely argue that insurance premiums would fall if more people took health insurance and fewer become ill. In other words, more people would be able to afford coverage if there were ways by which fewer people would become ill. No doubt, providing health insurance coverage for the aging population in developed countries is expensive because the elderly tend to suffer from chronic diseases, although it does not have to if healthcare providers utilized appropriate healthcare ICT, as indeed, should not, a wide variety of illnesses whether or not related to old age. A sedentary lifestyle, excessive alcohol use, smoking, illicit drug use, unhealthy eating habits, overweight and obesity, and shortage and misdistribution of healthcare professionals are other factors that increase health insurance prices, many of which are preventable, or possible to correct, again, an objective for which there is little doubt about how much healthcare ICT could help in achieving. Put differently, ICT could help in for example the primary, secondary, and tertiary prevention approaches that could reduce disease prevalence, and the morbidity, and mortality associated with many diseases, and facilitate the delivery of comprehensive, equitable, and accessible healthcare, cost-effectively, hence contain healthcare costs, and by extension, health insurance costs, private or public. In particular, by helping bring private health insurance costs down, more people would be able to afford it, in countries such as the US that relies primarily on private health insurance. To be sure, there are other factors involved in healthcare markets functioning optimally, which in effect is what needs to happen for consumers and taxpayers to not only be able to afford and access health services, but also to obtain the best value for their health care money. Achieving these goals would require appropriate changes in public policy in many countries, aimed at improving the productivity of the health system and quality of healthcare delivery, and in which healthcare ICT would feature prominently5.

Insurance reform is one of the important public policy changes required to promote the effective and efficient operations of healthcare markets. Improved information provision and utilization via the implementation of the necessary technologies would facilitate the implementation of these reforms, needed in both private and public health systems. However, any policy pronouncement on insurance reforms needs to be rooted in a thorough appraisal of salient issues pertaining to the health insurance industry. The role of private health insurance is supplemental in Canada and the UK, for examples, where Medicare and the National Health Service (NHS) provide comprehensive health services. Individuals only need private health insurance in these countries for services the publicly funded health systems do not cover, among other reasons. This is why only about 7 million (12%) people in the UK have private health insurance, a tenth of who, their employers fund. In Canada, people take coverage for services Medicare does not cover such as optometrist, dental, and podiatric services or need additional coverage for travel abroad. Private health insurance in the UK provides protection for curable, short-term health problems and as some contend, enables policyholders to jump the NHS queues to see consultants, receive faster diagnosis, surgery, and the newest medications. Even in the UK, the ideal of the NHS is to provide comprehensive health services to its peoples, and the use of private health insurance some would insist is an unintended consequence of the well-meaning government intention to improve the effectiveness of healthcare delivery in the country by introducing some semblance of free market operations in the country s health systems. Would it then not be necessary to introduce measures to discourage such activities as queue jumping by those who could afford private health insurance? One such measure is reducing wait times for receiving care, the time from one point to another on the continuum of care, and a major benchmark of a country s healthcare system, with which ICT could help in many ways. Saskatchewan province in Canada achieved this goal last year by simply publishing wait lists on an Internet website, thereby facilitating informed decision-making about treatment and lab testing options by patients and doctors, helping to optimize limited professional and hospital resources. This simple and cost-effective measure enabled the province with only 1093 GPs, and 403 specialists in 2005, reduce its wait lists by 3,200 in 2005 compared to 2004, according to data recently released by the province s Surgical Care Network, which collaborates with the Western Canada Waitlist Project. Ontario's Cardiac Care Network, which maintains and manages a veritable and comprehensive database on services such as cardiac surgery and angioplasty, and the British Columbia Surgical Waiting List Registry, which tracks and posts wait times data for all non-emergency surgical procedures by category on the government website, are other best practices in Canada. Data mining could also provide valuable analytics of systems utilization, segmented by variables such as demographics, for example patients ages, sex, even their races and countries of origins. As examples, diabetes is common among people of African descent, American Indians and Hispanics, to mention a few, and recessive genetic disorders among peoples with high rates of intermarriages among close relatives, both instances which could point to the extent of the need, for example, of pediatric surgical services, in locations with high populations of the latter. Telehealth, web-based and telephone consultations and treatment are other technologies that could help alleviate the shortage of healthcare professionals often contributory to the wait-lists problem in many countries. Electronic health records and other technologies are invaluable in gathering, collating and sharing patient information among healthcare professionals and healthcare facilities that could help in wait list management, and obviate the need to skip queues in the first place. Technology-enabled, evidence-based practice could help with standardizing wait times, and prioritizing the needs and urgency to treat patients on wait lists. Indeed, Canadian governments at F/ P/ T levels are taking the wait times issue seriously. At a First Ministers meeting in September 2004, the First Ministers agreed that each jurisdiction would set up comparable indicators of access to health care professionals, diagnostic and treatment procedures, with a report to their citizens by December 31, 2005. They also agreed to develop evidence-based benchmarks for medically acceptable wait times, beginning with cancer, heart, diagnostic imaging procedures, joint replacements, and sight restoration, by the end of 2005, through a process the FPT Ministers of Health would develop. The Ministers also wanted each jurisdiction to establish multi-year targets to achieve priority benchmarks by the end of 2007, to report yearly to their citizens on progress in meeting these targets, and to reduce wait times in priority areas such as cancer, heart, diagnostic imaging, joint replacements, and sight restoration by March 31, 2007. To underscore its commitment to reducing wait times, the Government of Canada provided an additional 41 billion dollars to Health over the next decade, including a 4.5 billion dollar *Wait Time Reduction Fund* for jurisdictional priorities use.

Insurers could reclassify illnesses from acute and curable to long-term and chronic, unceremoniously removing coverage for an illness previously covered, with sometimes-calamitous consequences for the policyholder. There are also issues with the concept of prevention, which technically private insurers abhor, insisting on coverage for treatment of conditions when they arise and their prevention. However, considering the different technical meanings of the word prevention in Medicine, for example, secondary prevention, which is the early diagnosis and prompt treatment of diseases, the issue, should hardly be contentious. How would private insurers view using tamoxifen, for example, which a large study to determine its effectiveness in reducing the risk in women at high risk for breast cancer, showed women who took the drug for up to 5 years (an average of 4 years) had 49% fewer diagnoses of invasive breast cancer than those who took a placebo? Private insurers might still view it as prevention, but clearly not public insurance, for which there would be enormous savings in future treatment costs and the dividend in lives saved, priceless. Other issues create disputes between the insured and insurers for example that of medications. Health insurers will not pay for experimental drugs and procedures, some claim, a loophole they exploit refusing to pay for such services even well after they have become standard practice. Some have even accused Health Maintenance Organizations (HMOs) in the US of unacceptable cost-containment practices such as having non-medical staff determine which services or medications to cover based on purely cost considerations. In the UK, insurers only approve the use of medications whose use in the NHS in England and Wales, the Institute for Health and Clinical Excellence, has approved, and some claim that the Institute has a conflict. They argue that because it is not only mandated to ensure that a drug works, but also to examine its cost/ benefit analysis and to ensure it is favorable to the NHS, it sometimes delays drug approval. There is no doubt that there could be many reasons for such delays, which many complain about in the US and Canada too, but ICT could help speed things up. In the US for example, the Food and Drug Administration (FDA), an agency of the U.S. Department of Health and Human Services (HHS), has to review all test results for new agents to ensure that products are safe and effective for specific uses in accordance with the law. This process starts when a research sponsor or pharmaceutical company deems a new agent promising in the lab, and applies for FDA approval via an Investigational New Drug (IND) application. Following are clinical trials, and when the sponsor considers there are enough data from the results of the trial to support a certain use for a drug, submits a New Drug Application (NDA) or a Biologics License Application (BLA) to FDA, for approval, the entire process on the average, about 15 years[6]. Often with millions of dollars invested in drug development by pharmaceutical companies, it is easy to see why they would be keen to see their drugs on pharmacy shelves as early as practicable, and indeed, why new drugs are often expensive. Nonetheless, the FDA usually has few if any reasons to be that in a hurry, ostensibly to ensure that consumers use safe and effective drugs. The FDA uses external and independent advisory committees of professionals and consumers for expert advice and guidance in determining whether to approve a new drug. Considering the amount of drug trial results and other documentation that these individuals must peruse, it is no wonder that the approval process does not happen too quickly. It is also unlikely far-fetched to imagine the chances of communication breakdowns between pharmaceutical companies, researchers testing the new agent in the field, the FDA, and its committee members, all of which a thorough analysis of the workflow and processes involved in these various communication and information-sharing pathways with resulting deployment of appropriate ICT could help rectify. Indeed, some would say that it should shock no one to find that some of these processes are still in the main, paper-based, with endless rims of paper passed from office to office, some snail-mailed, others lost in transit, and yet others stuck on someone s in-tray for weeks, when automating the entire process would save so much trouble. How many lives would speedy approval of a drug known to cure a certain type of cancer save, with health insurers changing its status from an experimental to an approved drug? Insurers do not also pay for pre-existing illnesses, except they have offered a moratorium of some number of symptom-free years, and progress in medical knowledge that may affect the classification of illnesses as being treatable or not. New treatments cost more, could increase claims, which invariably results in increased premiums, pricing some out, with the health subsidizing the ill. In the US for example, where but for insurance organized by employer-sponsored groups, private health insurance would be for many of these employees, as it is for many unemployed and self-employed people, unaffordable. Some think that employer-sponsored insurance gives employers unnecessary advantage in their dealings with their employees who seem to be overly depended on them for health insurance coverage, the reason Congress passed COBRA and other laws and enable the self-employed to claim tax deductions on health insurance premiums for which they pay. Another key issue with private health insurance has to do with billing, with insurers now keen on bill reviews by the insured to ensure the veracity of the claims healthcare providers submit for reimbursement, insurers rewarding the insured for recognizing undelivered services, sometimes with these claims hotly disputed by healthcare providers.

There are also issues with public health insurance, particularly as some contend, the increasing de-insurance of certain healthcare services as part of ongoing cost control and containment measures many governments are undertaking, including in Canada. The cost-containment measures governments across Canada took in the 1980s and 1990s led to major cutbacks in federal cash transfers for health care, education, and social services. The effects of these cutbacks on health included hospital closures and de-insurance of certain health services, and the emergence of some forms of private payment such as user fees, deductibles, and co-payments. Some would argue that Canadians are paying more for private health expenditures including prescription drugs, eye care, dental care, home care, long-term care, and non-physicians services today due to the lingering consequences of that era. The corresponding fact is that concerns about healthcare costs persist, and are even worse, with the country spending 9.6% of its gross domestic product (GDP) on health in 2002, projected at 10.1% in 2004, and rising. The question is what to do about it, as it is unlikely that the country could afford an indefinite increase in its health spending. The question becomes even more relevant in the context of the threat to its cherished Medicare by the recent Supreme Court ruling in Quebec giving legal backing to private health system in the province, a ruling that some fear the courts would replicate in other provinces and perhaps eventually countrywide. There would likely be profound changes in the healthcare status quo were this to happen. Trepidations on opposing sides of the public v. private health system debate continues, and include, for supporters of public insurance, noncompliance with the Canada Health Act, depletion of the public health system of scarce healthcare professionals, queue jumping and lengthening of the wait lists. For proponents of private insurance, there would be free reign of market forces, including fostering of competition, with eventual improvement in the quality of healthcare delivery, among others. There is no doubt that each side has its merits. However, regardless of the health system, cost would still be an issue, and although there would be a variety of alternative solutions to pursue in order to tackle the cost issue, many different and peculiar to the particular health system, both would benefit immensely in providing quality health services, cost-effective healthcare, implementing relevant healthcare ICT. Healthcare ICT could help a public insurance health system provide services that are more comprehensive and could make it more accessible to more peoples, even those living in remote or rural areas. It could help it achieve these goals more economically saving precious resources. By helping to reduce, wait lists for example, or the prevalence and morbidity of chronic, non-communicable diseases, or hospitalization rates, and lengths of hospital stays, healthcare ICT would make public insurance more sustainable, financially, at the same time, enhance the quality of care delivery, hence save many lives. Furthermore, by improving the quality of public health system, the private health system would have to improve their services to be competitive, not just with the public health system, but also internally, with pressure from private insurers, employers, and individuals purchasing health insurance on their own, not to mention government regulations that would likely mandate certain performance goals. With competition, private insurance premiums would likely fall, particularly with governments' preventive efforts on the healthcare services demand-reduction side, which again, healthcare ICT could play a significant role in actualizing. With the successes of preventive programs manifesting in reduced hospitalizations, and reappraisal of hospital structure, function, and distribution, and the increasing use of domiciliary and ambulatory care, some would argue for changes in Medicare. Currently, Medicare covers medications and supplies used by hospitalized patients, with individuals having to buy their medications and supplies once discharged from hospital or receiving treatment at home. They do so via private insurance or on their own, with many unable to who do not have private insurance or whose employer had not taken out one for, and cannot afford the medications and/ or supplies. Medicare, some would argue, needs reforms to rectify this problem, others for some other measure taken, as the hospital in its present form becomes an increasingly irrelevant and unwelcome cost driver in the healthcare delivery dynamics. Besides the clinical and public health fronts, health ICT deployment would facilitate structural reform of public health administration to relieve it of unwieldy bureaucracy, streamline its operations, and improve its effectiveness, much in keeping with the principles of "New Public Management" (NPM), which essentially involves adopting the "business operations mindset" in the public sector, to which Canada already subscribes.

Private health insurers also would benefit from implementing ICT to improve operations. By implementing such technologies, they could also help to reduce premium costs and increase the pervasiveness of private health insurance via improving their relationships with policyholders on the one hand and with healthcare providers and suppliers, on the other. Many insurance firms already use a variety of information systems technologies that simplify and facilitate tasks and work processes, but as some argue, the adoption of some of the newer technologies and ICT development models, for examples, service-oriented architectures (SOAs) and business-rules technologies would yield more remarkable yet cost-effective results, say, enterprisewide solutions, that could buoy profits. Proponents of these technologies argue that by standardizing and organizing application functionality, they create opportunities for insurance firms to meet and overcome contemporary business challenges such as generating revenues and profits, simultaneously reducing costs in an ever-competitive market place. There are concerns though that essentially setting aside in-depth business process analysis overrides the cost advantage in development time that an assemble rather than a business-process/ build model of IT development offers, in the long term, particularly in the healthcare industry. Thus, some would argue that offering a private insurer for example, billing management solutions may not help to address the various and intricate problems associated with medical billing that the insurance firm needs to solve in collaboration with their clients, and healthcare providers. It should be hardly debatable that insurers have as much at stake as other stakeholders in preventing sometimes-costly billing disputes, which would likely persist not using appropriate software and ICT due to not analyzing at all, or enough, medical billing processes, which incidentally are not necessarily generic, often varying in nature and complexity with the practice in question. Software vendors concerned about speed-to-market also use other code-reduction technologies such as, business process execution language (BPEL), which by developers actually writing business logic, and not merely coding, many contend facilitate the automation and seamless integration of multiple workflow processes, improving productivity, and saving costs. By helping to automate for example, reconciliation processes, which typically are heavily manual, multilevel, multi-departmental, and protracted, such approaches as BPEL save insurers much time and costs, their proponents insist. They also argue that so long as developers standardize the correct pieces, adhering to benchmarked levels of excellence, it becomes easier to Web-service the pieces, and establish an SOA, which once in place, business process automation follows. Furthermore, rather than examining code or laboring on systems integration, business automation, working with business concepts simply assembles the systems relations, essentially drastically reducing time from requirements analysis to code writing. Insurers could also establish and maintain business rules in applications with these technologies, facilitating speed-to-market for new products, and the efficiency of existing operations, for example, underwriting adjustments, which could give firms critical competitive edge in an industry where competitiveness increasingly hinges on innovative product offerings, creating more sophisticated underwriting workflow solutions and highly efficient processes. Insurers are using rules technology in ever-efficient manner, for example feeding every new client right from the point-of-sale system into an underwriting workflow solution, which tracks and manages the input automatically according to service level agreements with field agents. Such a system also enables staff to modify workflow to suit specific underwriters and modify underwriting resources, workflows, and service levels, for examples, in diverse company locations, within the country and abroad. With the need for insurers to be flexible, particularly in a constantly changing business environment such as the healthcare industry, where for example, it may be necessary to reclassify the status of a disease from acute to chronic, perhaps back to acute again each policy renewal year, business processes are also likely to change quite often. Insurers need to be able to capture these changes in order to determine the need or otherwise for software and ICT that could help improve the efficiency of the desired new processes, hence the importance of change- or configuration-management technologies in a potentially very dynamic development milieu. Insurers that ignore these important tasks risk system malfunction, and possibly a brush with the law for noncompliance with government regulations, in these days of HIPAA. The US Congress enacted the Health Insurance Portability and Accountability Act (HIPAA) in 1996, its first title, Title I to protect health insurance coverage for workers and their families in between or when they lose their jobs, its second, Title II, are the Administrative Simplification provisions. Title II requires the institution of national standards for electronic health care transactions and national identifiers for healthcare providers, health insurance plans, and employers. In 2005 alone, Michael Leavitt, who became HHS Secretary in the US in early 2005 made available $18.6 million in contracts to develop prototypes for a national healthcare information network and three contracts, altogether, $17.5 million to develop approaches to certifying healthcare IT tools, harmonizing health information standards and addressing variations in privacy and security laws among the states. To address the issue of making dissimilar health ICT systems communicate seamlessly, the government formed the 17-member American Health Information Community, a federally chartered advisory board whose memberships cut across government agencies, payers, providers, and patient groups. There is no doubt these measures highlight the commitment of the US government to facilitating health ICT adoption, interoperability of information systems, and the safety and confidentiality of patient information, in effect, leaving no reason why the insurance industry should do otherwise. Furthermore, unauthorized changes, on-the-fly-fixes, and such ad-hoc measures, for examples, would ultimately adversely affect system configuration. This could mean costly unplanned rework in the event of server failure, for example, not to mention its consequence for lost business, and perhaps more importantly, image and, by indicating possible lackadaisical handling of financial reporting systems, could be a violation in the US of the Sarbanes-Oxley Act of 2002. The Act, enacted in the wake of the Enron, Tyco, and other recent financial scandals that rocked the US corporate world, aims to protect investors by improving the accuracy and reliability of corporate disclosures. Insurers being key players in the healthcare industry owe it a moral duty to be part of the crusade to promote the widespread adoption of healthcare ICT in the industry, which has lagged behind other information-intensive industries such as banking, in utilizing the enormous potential of ICT to propel medical practice forward in a new age of relentless technological progress. This alignment would not only improve the quality of care delivery, and save innumerable lives, considering that in an age in which the service industry is pre-eminent, from whence over 50% of the wealth of nations in the developed world flows, could one ask why the single most important service of all seemingly continues to struggle with ICT adoption? The reasons are many and the insurance industry could collaborate with the healthcare industry to facilitate ICT adoption in the latter and higher diffusion in its own domain, for their mutual benefit.

Information is crucial to the efficient operations of the health insurance markets. Like the health industry, the insurance industry is information-intensive. Several salient issues beset the sharing and use of client information, in particular those of privacy and confidentiality. There is justifiable concern among the public regarding personal information falling into the wrong hands, and many corporate bodies have admitted that hackers have been able to access their purportedly secure databases, which makes these fears anything but irrational. The onus is on insurers to ensure the security of their databases, which means investing in cutting-edge ICT that would keep potential intruders at bay. Indeed, these issues are of such major concern that several US states plan to enact laws in 2006 to protect against the theft and misuse of personal information with commerce increasingly moving to the Internet. New Jersey and Virginia plan to illegalize making public anyone's Social Security number, Minnesota to require businesses that hold such information to notify clients promptly in the event of a breach of security. These new laws would complement current state and federal laws on information privacy and confidentiality in the US. Other developed countries also have such laws and many propose to enact and enforce more. Besides promoting public confidence in the operations of the industry, insurers should acknowledge that it is in their best interest to secure information rather than see doing so as a cost issue, as they may be preventing otherwise costly litigations downstream. It may also be necessary for some insurers to upgrade their information systems in order to accommodate the new processes that new state health laws may warrant. Missouri for example has established a prescription-drug program for lower-income seniors to pick up costs that the new federal Medicare prescription plan does not cover. Incidentally, millions of older Americans were able to access the new government-subsidized prescription drugs, which took effect on January 1, 2006, although some were not. The US federal government announced on December 22, 2005, that over a million of the 42 million Medicare beneficiaries had voluntarily signed up for the new prescription drug benefit, while 10.6 million had been enrolled automatically by the federal government or by health maintenance organizations. However, there have been complaints by pharmacists that they had problems confirming the eligibility of some individuals because Medicare's computers were not working properly, apparently jammed by the innumerable calls by people wanting to fill their prescriptions. Some pharmacists claim that up to a third of their low-income patients have been paying for their prescriptions, out-of-pocket, other pharmacists, loaning their clients, the medications, meantime, many clients at risk of not been able to receive their medications, their illnesses possibly worsening. These problems underscore the importance of not just implementing ICT but subjecting it to rigorous inspection, measurement, and configuration management during the development process to ensure building the right product, and further testing, measurement, and reliability growth modeling to ensure that developers built the right product, including real-life scenarios and independent quality assessment. To be sure, according to a report on Thursday January 05, 2006, in the *Arkansas Democrat-Gazette,* the Centers for Medicare and Medicaid Services (CMS) has increased the staffing to call centers and is updating a database that provides coverage information for beneficiaries to help address problems with the distribution of medications the new prescription drug benefit created. This new Medicare drug coverage is the largest expansion of the program in its 40-year history. Government is offering it via private insurance plans it is subsidizing, at a federal cost projected at $724 billion in the first decade. Unlike the customary Medicare, where the government offers a uniform package of benefits, with only trifling variations, many different plans, premiums, co-payments and covered drugs lists termed formularies, would be available with the new program. In general, there are two types of Medicare drug plans offered in 2006, the Medicare prescription drug plan, and the Medicare Advantage plan. The former covers just prescription drugs and nothing else. Offered by Medicare-approved private companies, up to 40 such plans offered in most states, they are preferable for those who require drug coverage, but would rather obtain their other benefits from the fee-for-service Medicare program. The latter, covers all Medicare benefits, including the new Medicare drug benefit. Often available alongside the former, also sponsored by private insurance companies, and include HMOs, PPOs, and private fee-for-service plans, these plans sometimes offer extra benefits but typically restrict enrollees choice of doctors. Massachusetts also recently signed into law, a bill to create an emergency plan to cover prescription drug costs for seniors and the disabled. Wisconsin has a broader-based health-care program for the working poor in order to provide prenatal care and delivery services to illegal immigrants and inmates, and Nevada now mandates insurance firms to cover cancer patients taking part in the earliest phase of clinical trials[7]. Insurers should adopt a strategic approach to viewing compliance to regulations, as a source of competitive advantage and not a burden, considering the potential for differentiation using ICT to accomplish this goal.

The need for insurers to seek competitive edge could not be more in today's industry milieu. Indeed, experts believe the more competition in a market, the healthier and more efficient it is. Besides the role of governments in seeking enabling environments for the poor, elderly, and the disabled to have health insurance, which in effect shrinks the market and accentuates competition, developments in the related industries such as finance, are likely going to heighten the stakes. Consider the announcement on January 4, 2005, officials of BancorpSouth Bank that the Tupelo, Mississippi-based, $11.5 billion asset banking firm has introduced a special Health Savings Account for individuals with high-deductible health plans, the BancorpSouth Health Savings Account (HSA). This is a special account established under the tax laws that enable eligible persons to save and pay for qualified health care expenses such as co-pays, hospital visits, prescription and some non-prescription drugs, and some insurance premiums for example those for long-term care that certain high-deductible health plans do not covers. The field of choices healthcare coverage for potential clients is likely to expand in future, with financial institutions, investments, trust and fiduciary services companies, and others not traditionally or strictly, within the insurance industry foraying into it, and creating an ever-increasing market competition. BancorpSouth Bank for example, demands that a client has a qualifying high-deductible health plan (HDHP) in order to open an HSA. By offering savings on medical coverage, more control of personal health care, substantial tax benefits, and a novel approach to invest for retirement, an HSA, is opening new vistas for competition in the health insurance industry. Competitors would have to meet or surpass the benefits of an HSA for examples, tax-deductibility, tax-free withdrawals to purchase qualified health services, rolling over unused funds into the following year s accounts with taxes deferred, or even being able to write checks for service payment with on a savings account. Significantly, while the bank allows clients to choose their preferred HDHP insurance provider, it offers a unitary solution for the HDHP via its insurance subsidiary, which it undeniably favors. There is no doubt that health insurers could improve the efficiency of their processes and service new ones designed to ease clients experience doing business with them, and facilitate communications and information sharing with their partners and agents in the field, implementing appropriate ICT. The benefit of so doing might not only be desirable for the industry, but in fact, might be in keeping with the need for the industry to survive, as an examination of potential events in other sectors of the economy, for example taxation, reveals. Some advocate tax reforms as key to market efficiency, including the healthcare market. Indeed, in the case of the US, some experts believe that tax reform is inevitable, given the amount of money going into funding health insurance. According to CMS estimates, the Medicare prescription drug benefit will cost $724 billion in its first decade, and about $2 trillion in its next. Some predict that Medicare would have about $30 trillion in unfunded obligations over the next quarter century, a third linked with the prescription drug benefit. These figures had some asking if the plan is sustainable, where the money would come from, other than dramatic increases in taxes, others querying who pays them. These issues are clearly going to bear significantly on the future of health insurance. It is paradoxical that the fiscal impact of the longevity many crave has become the source of so much discord. This is not just regarding its effect on health but in the realm of welfare in general. Countries such as the UK, Australia, and new Zealand, which have all initiated profound health reforms, including the introduction of varying degrees of free-market operations in their health systems have, nonetheless, fought shy of tapping non-tax revenue sources for health financing, something Canada so far also abhors. The recent disagreement between the British Prime Minister and his Chancellor of the Exchequer over the report of the Turner Commission on Pensions, underlines the continuing search for solutions to financing the country's social and healthcare problems. Lord Turner in his November 2005 report recommended increasing the retirement age from 65 years to 67 years as part of pension reforms, which the Chancellor did not favor, branding it unsound and unaffordable. The Chancellor, Mr. Gordon Brown, allegedly wrote a letter to Lord Turner, pointing out that Government might have to cut the real value of the pension credit, an important policy for aiding poorer pensioners, in as short a period as three years from now. By linking pension credit increase with that of earnings as Turner proposed, rather than as Brown did that of price index, experts believe the Chancellor's fears about the source of money to fund state pension are genuine. Governments in developed countries, most with an increasingly aging population and a corresponding need for a variety of healthcare services, not just for seniors but other citizens, would have to start looking at the interplay of relevant factors in order to be able to guarantee health services provision without committing fiscal hara-kiri. In fact, some would argue for full legislative support for such moves as that announced by the American Federation of Unions-Congress of Industrial Organizations (AFL-CIO) on Thursday January 05,

2006, that large corporations spend a percentage of their payroll on employee health insurance. Incidentally, the Maryland legislature passed such a bill in 2005, but its Governor vetoed it, and it now awaits override by the legislature. AFL-CIO plans to pursue laws, the so-called "Fair Share Health Care" bills, in 31 states that would require that the largest private employers in a state, those with over 10,000 workers, devote 8% to 11% of their payroll to health insurance or make a payment a state insurance fund. Others would caution, however, about driving corporations whose existence is important to the overall health of the economy into bankruptcy by too-overly draconian legislation. Indeed, some would even argue further that the problem is with insuring the employed, as most corporations already have some form of insurance for their workers at least in the US, compared to their competitors in Europe, hence that the proposed laws are misdirected. To be sure, some labor unions seem to acknowledge the problem with being too heavy-handed on the corporations. UAW members in November, and December 2005, ratified an agreement with GM, and Ford, respectively that would require union retirees to pay monthly premiums and annual deductibles for health insurance to help reduce the firm's health care costs, although UAW retirees did not participate in the votes, and some are already contesting the agreement. In the event of such laws coming to effect in the US, it is possible that labor unions in other countries would follow suit. What consequence would this have for insurers though, particularly for their relationships with employers, who might be a little keener to know where their money is going? What would this also mean for competition among insurers? Would it consolidate the hegemony of major carriers or would it, for example, as stipulated probably by legislation, open up markets for smaller, local insurers? How would brokers assessing healthcare providers, on the bases of their service offerings, standards, type and qualifications of professionals, use of health ICT, and other yardsticks to assist individuals seeking private healthcare services, a development becoming more commonplace even in Canada, where most health insurance is still publicly funded, influence competition among insurers? This and novel business activities, related some albeit remotely to the insurance industry, might turn out to be crucial drivers of competition in the future health insurance industry. Corporations are unlikely to be the only ones to bear part of the ever-increasing healthcare costs. With the US senior population expected to double from 35 million to 70 million over the next 20 years, for example, in part, because the health of individuals aged 65 years and above has been increasingly buoyant since the 1980s, some would insist that a major paradigm shift in health services delivery is also necessary. Some would argue further that it is actually imperative in order to contain healthcare costs, while ensuring comprehensive service provision. According to recent forecasts by the National Institute on Aging and the American Association of Homes and Services for the Aging, seniors care would shift from nursing homes toward more support-based services and ICT that allow domiciliary patient monitoring. This would undoubtedly necessitate changes to Medicare and Medicaid reimbursement schedules for such services. How such developments would play out in the health insurance industry would likely be quite dramatic, both in its impact on competition, and on the profitability, if not even on the very survival of some of the insurance firms.

References

1. Available at:
http://www.cbsnews.com/stories/2004/06/25/health/main626132.shtml
Accessed on January 1, 2006

2. Available at: http://www.familiesusa.org/issues/uninsured/
Accessed on January 1, 2006

3. Available at: http://www.familiesusa.org/issues/uninsured/
Accessed on January 1, 2006

4. Moran, D.W., Whence and whither Health Insurance? A Revisionist History
Health Affairs, Vol. 24, Issue 6, 1415-1425

5. Making Markets Work: Five Steps To A Better Health Care System
John F. Cogan, R. Glenn Hubbard, and Daniel P. Kessler Health Affairs, Vol. 24, Issue 6, 1447-1457

6. DiMasi, J.A. (2001). New drug development in the United States 1963-1999. Clinical Pharmacology and Therapeutics May; 69(5); Tufts Center for the Study of Drugs Development, Tufts University; adapted from Pharmaceutical Research and Manufacturers of America.

7. Available at: http://www.philly.com/mld/philly/news/nation/13531424.htm
Accessed on January 5, 2006

8. Available at: http://www.chron.com/cs/CDA/printstory.mpl/prn/texas/3565714
Accessed on January 5, 2006

9. Available at:
http://www.ctv.ca/servlet/ArticleNews/mini/CTVNews/20060103/ELXN_martin_h
ealth_060104/20060104?s_name=election2006&no_ads=
Accessed on January 5, 2006

ICT and Health Cost Benefits

Lawmakers in Maryland, USA, first approved legislation that would require companies with more than 10,000 employees to boost spending on health care on April 5, 2005. The law mandates such companies to spend at least 8 percent of their payroll on health benefits, or put the money directly into the state's health program for the poor. The State Governor, Robert L. Ehrlich Jr. (R), vetoed that legislation. The legislators overrode the Governor on January 14, 2006, and passed the bill. Buoyed by this development, workers' unions are vowing to push for similar laws in at least 30 other states, although reports indicate that retailing and restaurant chains, which are the most susceptible to any state law mandating coverage because they employ many low-income workers, are waging a counter-offensive to prevent legislators from passing such laws outside Maryland. Indeed, the National Retail Federation, the National Restaurant Association, and the International Franchise Association have formed an alliance pursuant to this goal. With the cost of providing workers with health care rising faster than that of any other component of employee benefits, and if left unchecked, the costs of health insurance expected to guzzle the profits of many such companies in as few as five years, these must be troubling times for many companies. The recent health insurance fiasco at General Motors and Ford, which some would argue threatened the very survival of these companies, and which both management and workers' unions had to resolve as promptly as they could, highlight the nature and seriousness of the problem for all parties. It is no wonder many companies are seeking ways to control these costs, measures some firms have taken including shifting costs to their employees, or improving their sourcing, but none would argue that the problem requires all-inclusive and sustainable solutions. The question is what are these solutions? How could companies control their health benefit costs? Experts proffer measures such as in-depth knowledge of the drivers and other critical factors underlying their health insurance costs and their employees' health priorities, consolidate insurance programs to cut down costs, and giving providers, incentives to promote employee wellness, among others, but could healthcare ICT also help? Some contend that the bill targets Wal-Mart, the giant retailer with over 5000 stores, $285 billion worldwide and over 15,000 workers in Maryland alone. However, others point out that Johns Hopkins University, Giant Food, and defense contractor Northop Grumman Corp. also have enough employees to fall under the bill s requirements, either the 8 percent threshold for for-profit employers or the 6 percent, for nonprofit organizations. Others see the bill as retrogressive and one whose possible consequences of reduced investment, even de-investment in the state could backfire on hunt Maryland workers perhaps even worsen the health problems of laid-off workers and their dependants in the state. This raises the question of the options the affected companies indeed, have. Wal-Mart, for example, has been experiencing a rash of negative publicity for some time. Its labor practices, including charges of gender discriminations, are under intense scrutiny, because of which the firm faced a number of lawsuits. In 2004, the company agreed to pay $11 million to settle claims regarding the use illegal immigrants by one of its cleaning contractors, and the Vice Chairman Thomas M. Coughlin resigned sequel to allegations of questionable use of about $500,000 in company funds. Some industry analysts argue that the firm s image problems would no doubt take its toll on its profits sooner than later. Furthermore, the firm s future and its ability to continue to expand are inseparable, which is why its loss of several bids to build stores in locations in the US, where many local governments have also passed zoning rules complicating the company s expansion programs, foreshadows hard days ahead for the company. It is therefore understandable that Wal-Mart, which claims that more than three-fourths of its 1.3 million U.S. employees has health insurance coverage, either through the company, a spouse, or a government program would not welcome the ruling by the Maryland legislators. It seems likely though, that the company would start looking for ways to reduce its health benefit costs, particularly as there are indications that other state legislators might take a cue from their colleagues in Maryland. Some would argue that employers have even more urgent reasons to do so because not only are companies already confronting a harsh economic climate and persistent margin pressures, employers are bearing increasing portions of the escalating healthcare costs. What is more, and uncharacteristic of the private sector which thrives on ensuring the judicious spending on every dollar it expends, companies are bearing these costs in a milieu of a dearth of overriding benchmark of practices, with resulting inconsistencies in the quality of healthcare delivery, among jurisdictions, even among hospitals. What then are the options that Wal-Mart and other companies that these laws would affect have? In particular, should these companies not be seeking ways to exploit the many benefits healthcare ICT offers that could in the short-and long-terms help control health benefits costs?

It seems for these companies reasonable to start by examining what the drivers of healthcare costs are. Indeed, not only companies are interested in doing so. Many government establishments are introducing regulations, and local governments, bylaws, restricting cigarette smoking, for example, in public buildings, including hospitals, and in bars and restaurants, because of the research evidence of the association between cigarette smoking and certain health problems such as chronic bronchitis, emphysema, even lung cancer. Some companies are also taking other measures, some albeit criticized as being discriminatory, such as demanding that their workers lose weight, or not being keen to employ overweight or obese persons. Such measures clearly also rest on research evidence of the link between obesity and chronic health problems such as diabetes, these examples, the companies consider important drivers of health benefits costs, no doubt. Indeed, two recent studies published in the January 11, 2005 issue of the Journal of the American Medical Association, noted that being overweight or obese in middle age, even if an individual does not have risk factors such as high blood pressure or high cholesterol, increases the chances of that person developing heart disease later in life. In the first study, researchers examined data on 17,643 men and women between the ages of 31 and 64 included in the Chicago Heart Association Detection Project in Industry, and divided them into groups according to how high were their risks for heart diseases. The groups were, the low risk group, those that did not smoke, and had normal blood pressure and cholesterol readings; and the moderate risk group, who also did not smoke, but may have had slightly elevated blood pressure or cholesterol levels. There were also the intermediate risk group, who had one of the following risk factors, current smoking, high cholesterol, or high blood pressure; the elevated risk group, who had two risk factors; and highest-risk group, who had all three risk factors for heart disease. The average follow-up period was 32 years. The researchers found the risk of death from heart disease to be 43 percent higher for obese people in the low-risk group compared to people of normal weight and 2.1 times higher for obese people, in the moderate-risk group. The risk of hospitalization was also higher for obese people, in the low-risk group, who had a 4.2 times greater risk of hospitalization for heart disease. Indeed, the adverse effects of obesity transcend the cardiovascular domain, with a recent study conducted in China, by researchers at Vanderbilt University in Nashville, Tennessee, and published in the January 15, 2006 issue of the American Journal of Epidemiology, supporting previous Western studies that obesity also compromises the survival of breast cancer patients. Some experts contend that this is because it makes it more difficult to diagnose breast cancer, others that excess body fat, by increasing estrogen, and testosterone levels, and possibly those of some other hormones, helps speed up the growth and spread of breast tumors. Yet other scientists believe that obesity increases the risk of developing breast cancer in the first place, the hormonal effects of extra body fat thought the mediators. Do these findings not suggest that interventions aimed at weight control may have a significant effect on not just breast cancer incidence but also on surviving the disease? Do these studies not confirm that obesity is a real public health crisis and one in which not only companies, but also individuals and indeed, all healthcare stakeholders ought to show keen interest? A recent study published in the January 17, issue of the Canadian Medical Journal shows that the prevalence of overweight and obesity in Canada have increased between 1985 and 2003. In particular, the prevalence of class III or the most extreme form of obesity, with body mass index (BMI), the ratio of weight in kilograms, to height in meters squared, over 40, from 0.4% to 1.3% between 1990 and 2003, a 225% increase. These figures mirror those reported for the US, a 175% increase from 0.8% to 2.2% between 1990 and 2000₁. Furthermore, with over one billion people in the world overweight and, at the current rate projected to be 1.5 billion by 2015, according World Health Organization (WHO) estimates, and of the current total, over 300 million obese, hence at substantial risk of heart disease, stroke, type 2 diabetes, respiratory problems and some cancers, should this problem not concern all stakeholders? With obesity spreading rapidly in developing countries, including Africa and the western Pacific islands of Nauru and Tonga reputed to have the highest percentage rates of obesity in the world the problem is indeed, global. What does this mean for productivity, for companies that have global operations, even if they did not have to worry about health insurance in some of their operational bases? Should they still not be interested in finding solutions to the problems? With the sales of just one anti-obesity drug, the latest, Sanofi-Aventis SA's Acomplia, or rimonabant, expected to receive FDA approval as early as February 2006, estimated at over $3 billion a year, should software and ICT firms also be thinking of developing innovative products that could help people shed weight, via excise and diet? Could there be simple but effective exercise video programs recorded and played back on cellular phones or iPods, that workers could do in their offices for a few minutes a few times a day, of course listening with mini-headphones so as not to distract co-workers? Indeed, ICT is moving at a fast pace, creating immense the opportunities for healthcare. It is not just possible to watch downloadable audio and video clips on mobile devices one could also watch live, streaming video, even live TV programs on the cellular phone or Treo Smartphone, via MobiTV services. Another device called the Slingbox makes it possible for someone to watch his or her TV programming from any location, from a different room, house, even anywhere in the world by simply turning virtually any Internet-connected PC into a personal TV. There is also EchoStar's portable video player, the PocketDish, which enables someone to download, to record, and play content from a variety of sources such as a PC or Mac, digital cameras, mass-storage devices, digital video players, camcorders, and VCRs. It is compatible with most current TV sets and consumer electronic devices, and possible to dock to select DVRs, using a USB 2.0 connection for very fast video transfers of Dish programming to a portable device. The much faster, imminent N-standard would also create immense opportunities for wireless networking in the health sector, although the rush to market the so-called pre-N devices is creating its own standards and interoperability problems. What would companies benefit encouraging their workers to own and use these devices? Such devices could also facilitate workers contact with their healthcare providers and encourage reporting of health problems, hence facilitate prompt treatment, reducing morbidities, even mortalities, and health costs. To illustrate this point, a recent study conducted in Canada, and published in the January 2006 edition of the Canadian Journal of Psychiatry showed that persons with suicidal ideation are much less likely to contact healthcare professionals except they also have depression. This finding is disturbing but even more so is that it showed that 2 out of 3 suicidal persons did not have depression, considering that some of these individuals might end up actualizing their suicidal thoughts, with depression eventually developing due to lack of prompt treatment2. The results of this study have important implications for mental health needs assessments and resource allocation. Such multimedia healthcare ICT devices as those mentioned earlier could encourage individuals to seek help knowing that it is just a click away. They could also facilitate effective treatments for these persons such as crisis intervention, supportive therapy, and even cognitive therapy, without the need for physical contact with their doctors or mental health professionals. There is no gainsaying what the individuals concerned, their families, the companies they work for, and society at large could save in human and material costs, if individuals had and used these ICT devices to contact appropriate healthcare professionals, as and when necessary. Indeed, not only should companies encourage workers to use such devices, they should reward somehow, healthcare providers that have wellness programs or encourage workers to embrace them. In centralizing their insurance programs, which would also help reduce costs, companies should consider contracting with insurers that also have such compensation programs for providers. One way to compensate providers could be helping them finance healthcare ICT implementation. A recent Canadian study showed that mental illness costs Canadian businesses $33 billion annually in disability payouts. This study no doubt confirms that companies would save significantly in health benefits costs, being active in promoting a healthy workforce, including encouraging their workers to use healthcare ICT devices such as those mentioned earlier, and other relatively inexpensive, and easy to use, consumer healthcare ICT products that could substantially reduce morbidities3. Considering the potential market for such devices, would it not be surprising if software and ICT vendors paid little attention to developing innovative consumer health ICT products? Yet, some would insist that this seems to be the case. Instructive also are the findings of the second study on overweight and obesity that the chances are that a person is not receiving the appropriate treatment that is overweight or obese, or have other factors that put him or her at high risk for heart disease or stroke. This was a study of 70,000 people from 44 countries. All study participants had known arterial diseases, such as heart disease, stroke, or peripheral artery disease, and many were overweight or obese. Most were not on treatment, despite being at high risk for further problems, for example high cholesterol (70%). Eighty percent were not on anti-clotting medications, and 50 percent had poorly managed high blood pressure. What do these figures say for increasing morbidities and mortalities, and for rising health costs? Why are these people untreated anyway? Is it cost-related, is it due to noncompliance by the patient, or is it the GP or primary care physician, the first healthcare contacts of most of these patients, who is unaware of the current guidelines by each specialty, hence do not recognize the gravity of their patients health problems and the need to treat them appropriately and adequately? Indeed, with regard to the specialties, is there a silo-mentality that needs addressing among specialists, for example, that precludes the proper recognition of the need for conceptualizing heart attacks, and strokes, even if managed customarily by cardiologists and neurologists, as indicative of a pervasive cardiovascular pathology, hence approach their management from a collaborative perspective? What role could healthcare ICT play in facilitating such collaboration, and indeed, in tackling the various other issues mentioned as possible reasons for the non-or inadequate treatment of these individuals? Are these not also issues that companies need to focus on in their bid to drive down health benefits costs? Should they not be keener therefore, to understand how the use healthcare ICT could drive down costs due to these drivers? Companies could indeed, be more proactive regarding their employees health, instituting internal measures to improve their workers health, via the use of cutting-edge technologies without necessarily cutting into work times, or compromising productivity, but rather enhance, eventually, their employees health and the quality of their work. For example, they could encourage healthy eating habits by providing their employees multimedia health sessions, watched in departmental common rooms periodically, or presented by commissioned health or nutrition experts, as part of an internal health and fitness program. Another aspect of which could also be session exercises led by a fitness expert or presented on video that workers could perform even by their office desks, not to mention ergonomic measures to prevent health problems, for examples, in the joints, bones, and eyes, in workers that spend a lot of time at their desks working on computers for example. Such healthcare ICT-based diet and exercise initiatives could no doubt improve workers health, and indeed, operational efficiencies, and cut health benefits costs in the long term. Another company-wide initiative is for management to identify the sources of and reduce the amount of stress workers experience at work, part of the stress-reduction effort for example including providing compartmentalized, special relaxation rooms where workers could listen to soft, soothing music, or watch multimedia stress reducing pictures or video clips, or read a book, during coffee or lunch breaks. Many firms might be wary of the costs of these amenities and of the technologies involved, including the costs of implementing and maintaining them. True, the investment could be significant, but is it justifiable? Would the benefits that accrue from these initiatives for both the workers and the company not outweigh their costs in the long term?

To be sure, there are no easy solutions to the high health benefits costs companies currently face, in fact, the situation is anything but easy, considering that the federal governments in many countries spend billions of dollars on healthcare, spending increasing, companies paying a significant amount of these costs. This means that an appraisal of the entire health system would be necessary in order to put the problems in proper perspective and to facilitate finding the solutions to them. Even if the solutions are yet fuzzy, that healthcare ICT would play a crucial role in solving the problems is not in doubt. By automating and optimizing processes, healthcare ICT improves productivity, and via the power of the Internet, it facilitates communication and information sharing among a variety of stakeholders including healthcare providers, insurers, employers, suppliers, and patients and employees. Could these and other functionalities of healthcare ICT create opportunities for external initiatives that could help employers control health benefits costs? Do these initiatives require collaboration between employers and the other stakeholders in health for them to materialize? How could companies ensure such collaboration? Companies first need to understand that they cannot detach the health-costs problems that they face from that of the health industry as a whole, an industry that guzzles 15% of the gross domestic product (GDP) of the US, and spending on which continues to rise. Thus, companies should also want to know why health spending keeps rising, after all, they are paying a significant amount of these costs and those of them that employ more than 10,000 workers might be paying much more in due course, at least in Maryland. It is paradoxical that healthcare ICT, better still, the lack of it, is one important reason for the rising costs of healthcare in many countries, and it is not difficult to see why this is so. As previously mentioned, there are wide variations in service provision in many countries. Efforts to prevent diseases, in particular, those with known causative links, are appallingly inconsistent, some jurisdictions, with more advanced preventive and health promotion programs than others, the differences often in the intensity and sophistication of implemented healthcare ICT, which is important to achieving the goals of such efforts. Indeed, some jurisdictions are averse to the idea of mass health education campaigns, preferring piecemeal target programs. The latter approach is certainly suitable for some more localized, disease conditions but does research evidence suggesting that certain diseases, which might have been localized are now of such prevalence that they are almost creating a public health crisis not imply that they are rife for massive public education campaigns? Should there not be some standard, cross-country measures of determining the thresholds for such status change? Indeed, healthcare systems globally confront increasing pressure to develop health policy and program initiatives that reallocate more institutional resources to public health and community-based programming, and to develop novel, cost-effective, and public health services at local, provincial, state, and federal levels. Services to prevent diseases and promote physical, mental, and emotional wellbeing, for example via infectious disease surveillance and control, disease prevention with vaccination programs for example, health campaigns to promote wellness and healthy living, and population health analyses, among others, would certainly help reduce spiraling health costs in the long term. The success of these services depend in the main on the use of appropriate healthcare ICT, including among others data management and communication systems, and cutting-edge data mining systems, expert systems, artificial neural networks (ANN), Internet, mobile, and broadband technologies, and electronic health record systems. Yet, most countries health dollars still fund hospital services and prescription drugs and in the U.S. administrative costs of private health insurance as well. There is little doubt that the reallocation of resources to fund the necessary healthcare IT infrastructure necessary for information exchange among the various agencies responsible for these public health activities would create the enabling environment for the success of the prevention programs initiated by various jurisdictions. This would contribute overall to reducing disease prevalence, morbidities, and mortalities, and lowering health costs, including for employers. The dividends for companies supporting public health and disease prevention programs, at least in their jurisdictions, and efforts to facilitate health ICT diffusion, support that might be for government agencies, regulations, and programs, and for healthcare providers, might not be immediate, but it makes strategic sense to do so. It might seem to be a matter of social and legal responsibility for example, for firms in the agro-business and veterinary sectors to support and comply with government policies, initiatives, and regulations to prevent an imminent avian flu pandemic. However, it is not difficult to see the enormous costs not only such companies, but also others, and the world economy would incur in the event of such a pandemic. There are also inconsistencies in service provision due to either a lack of or adherence to evidence-based benchmarks of care, among other reasons. Employers, and indeed, government and individual purchasers of health services ought to have a say in rectifying this problem, which is a major reason for escalating healthcare costs. Where there are no standards of practice, there is likely to be and there are indeed service variations, and that means some services are inferior to others. Now, this does not only translate to purchasers receiving those inferior services, perhaps for which they might even be paying more than those who are receiving better services are, being short-changed, such mediocre services could only worsen health, prolong suffering, and increase health costs, but for who? Companies could therefore reduce health benefit costs by ensuring that their workers receive qualitative and comprehensive healthcare in keeping with their investments in health insurance. This not only requires that the health plans that companies patronize secure the services of healthcare providers that meet certain professional standards of care, including the implementation and use of healthcare ICT to facilitate and assure the quality of services but that the health plans themselves have appropriate ICT to ensure accurate and secure billing management for example. Could employers in fact not shun payers that do not and seek the services of those that implement ICT? It is indeed, inevitable for payers, in particular, health plans, to be more actively involved in ICT diffusion and related programs in the health sector. Some conceive of this participation in the ambit of regional health information organizations (RHIO), which some contend is the bedrock of the planned National Health Information Network (NHIN) in the US. Proponents argue that health information sharing is crucial more so in these days of pay-for-process and pay-for-performance programs, and consumer-directed healthcare, and that companies need to facilitate this process as part of their efforts to reduce health benefits costs. Health plans need to be able to communicate with physicians at the point of care

(POC), which such regional health information systems would facilitate, rather than have a retroactive pay-for-performance program, for example, and indeed, also need to communicate with consumers prior to and the POC. These the argument goes are essential requirements for the increasing market shift toward consumer-directed health plans, up to 8 percent of payers' portfolio in 2006, and projected to grow to 20% next year, to succeed. Other industry pundits see things differently, for example, those that argue for payer-based health records, although all agree on the importance of deploying information systems in contemporary healthcare delivery. In fact, there is consensus that besides companies insisting on payers utilizing healthcare ICT in care management, with possible sanctions such as seeking vendors elsewhere, government regulations might leave payers with few options. In any case, not many payers would argue that embracing the ideas of electronic medical records, and personal health records, and implementing appropriate healthcare ICT that enables them to exploit the functionalities of these various information portals would not be cost-effective in the end. Neither would many that by facilitating communication and information sharing between payers, providers and consumers, such healthcare ICT would not result in safer, more qualitative treatments, substantially mitigate business-related risks such as faulty billings, minimize time to market, and improve operational efficiencies, and administrative costs among others. Would these not reduce morbidities, rates of physician visits, and prevent costs passed on to consumers and by extension for those whose employers sponsor their health insurance, the employers?

It is not that a payer-led electronic health network is panacea for all the problems between plans and providers, some in fact scowl at the idea of payer data transformation to replace medical history. On the other hand, chief information officers and technical personnel in general, seem unenthusiastic about forfeiting their immediate concerns for building electronic health record systems for their health organizations that would boost their ranking than collaborating in a regional platform to share information with their competitors. Yet others believe that such efforts are less expensive than building the technology and governance structures for a RHIO. However, all would probably concede that competition aside, the National Health Information Network in the US and Canada s National Electronic Health Records Program administered by Canada Health

Infoway, are examples of health ICT initiatives at the highest government level that other countries should emulate. Among other reasons for embracing such initiatives, they no doubt provide the essential technological infrastructure for a standardized, comprehensive, and interoperable, technological platform for electronic health record systems nationwide that assures the continuity of care. Furthermore, it is also reasonable to assert that any country that is serious about reducing healthcare costs should be equally staid about providing its citizens with qualitative healthcare, and all agree that healthcare ICT diffusion is vital for achieving these objectives, which ICT could also help companies achieve. Differences in approaches to implementation notwithstanding therefore, companies need to remain steadfast in their conviction of the important role that healthcare ICT could play in reducing health benefit costs. They should also recognize the need to support whichever initiative or approach ensures that payers and providers alike implement the necessary healthcare ICT, that would improve the health of workers, and yield health costs savings for the companies. Chronic diseases are increasingly prevalent in developed countries such as the US and Canada, as correspondingly are the costs of treating them and their economic burden on society. Health care consumed 16 percent of the gross domestic product of the US in 2004, for example, slightly higher than the figure of 15.6% for 2003, which means that more of every dollar of output by the US goes into healthcare, and companies, now mandated to contribute even more to these healthcare costs. Should companies not be keen to follow what is really happening in the health sector, why more money is going into healthcare, particularly as they are responsible for paying some of this money? A recent, prevalence-based cost-of-illness (COI) study of the economic burden off schizophrenia, another typically chronic disease, in Canada4, showed that the economic burden of the disorder on the country is substantial. In spite of significant progress in drug therapy and the programs and services patients with schizophrenia can access, the economic burden of schizophrenia in Canada remains high, estimated direct healthcare and non-healthcare costs CAN$2.02 billion in 2004. The 374 deaths, mostly premature mortalities, attributed to schizophrenia plus the high unemployment rate due to the disorder amounting to a further productivity morbidity and mortality loss estimate of CAN$4.83 billion, with overall cost estimate in 2004 being CAN$6.85 billion, attributable mostly, as much as 70%, to morbidity-related productivity losses. The figures for 1996 were, CAN$1.12 billion, CAN$1.23 billion, and CAN$2.35 billion, respectively5. Even if most employed patients with schizophrenia, are usually in subsidized employment or earn much less than most others, should employers not be interested to ensure that those that work for them receive appropriate treatment in order to minimize morbidities and reduce costs? Should employers indeed, not be concerned about the wide variations in care provision, and in costs in countries that have private health insurance, and even in outcomes of this and other chronic disorders, and of illnesses in general? Would healthcare ICT not help with setting standards of care, promoting evidence-based practice, care monitoring, and evaluation and in facilitating the information sharing basic to achieving these quality levels? Would attention to these and related issues not help contain the increasing health costs of chronic diseases, which are becoming ever commoner? Would companies not be saving costs supporting preventive efforts to reduce the prevalence of these and in particular, preventable chronic diseases? How could the Internet help in this regard? In the US, health spending on doctor visits, hospital stays, and drugs, among other health needs, increased by 7.9 percent after an 8.2 percent increase in 2003, growth actually slowing slightly. These figures, released in a report published in the January 2006 edition of Journal Health Affairs, by economists at the National Center Statistics Group, a component of Centers for Medicare and Medicaid Services (CMS,) the US agency in charge of the country s insurance programs for the poor, elderly and disable, were telling. They showed that total health spending was $1.87 trillion in 2004, or approximately, $6,280 per person, almost twice 1993 s, $916.5 billion, but also a slight but significant slowing in the growth of health spending between 2003 and 2004. The reasons for this slowing include patients and health insurers purchasing cheaper generic and over-the-counter drugs, increasing mail-order dispensing, trend and decreased use of some drugs due to safety concerns. Indeed, spending growth on prescription drugs dropped by 2 percent from the year before to $188 billion, private sector efforts mostly responsible. In fact, not a few insurance firms now offer lower fees for patients who choose the less costly generic drugs. Should companies not benefit from these developments too? Should they not be interested to know what effects these developments would have on the overall quality of healthcare delivery among their workers? Even insurers want to cover procedures and medications that work, which evidence shows result in better outcomes, hence their preference in the US for a pay-for-performance system, as opposed to the current reimbursement system, which they see as rewarding providers for whatever they deem needed done for patients. ICT could help with benchmarking practices hence help to establish the connection between best practices and improved outcomes, thereby facilitating the implementation of a pay-for-performance system, harmonizing costs, while improving the quality of care delivery, with neither workers nor their employers losing out. Encouraging physicians to implement healthcare ICT does not mean giving them orders, one of the main complaints of some against the Managed Care Organizations in the US such as Preferred Provider Organizations (PPOs), and Exclusive Provider Organizations (EPOs), but in particular, the Health Maintenance Organizations (HMOs). Physicians would likely increasingly embrace the necessary healthcare ICT that would enable them provide the best, evidence-based care, although some would argue, unlikely that they would seek accurate, timely, and unbiased information from insurance firms the very reason some do not think the idea of payer-led electronic health network mentioned earlier would work. Some experts are in fact suggesting the emergence in future of third-party information brokers that would assemble and link industry data and information for real-time sharing among interested parties. Companies have a major role to play in promoting the use of ICT by providers and would have to be involved actively in finding solutions to some of the thorny issues providers and payers bicker over, most of which remain unresolved. By so doing, companies would be paving the way for uniform and qualitative healthcare delivery, which would translate into reduced benefit costs in the end.

WellPoint Inc., the largest health insurer in the US recently invested $40 million to encourage its in-network physicians to implement IT and start "e-prescribing," what many believe should be what insurance firms, should be doing in order to facilitate the progression toward an IT-enabled, evidence-based health care system. The insurer is providing its in-network doctors free, a desktop or "e-prescribing" unit for Internet connectivity, which the firm holds is the first step toward doing away with the paper-based system most healthcare providers still use. Interestingly, and despite being free, only 19, 500 of the 26,000 doctors contacted accepted the gift, and 2,700, the e-prescribing package, with just 150 of them using the technology to any significant extent. Does this not show that much needs done to change end-user attitudes? Does it not show that implementing technology is not all healthcare ICT diffusion into the core of medical practice would take? It is not at all surprising that many doctors still view healthcare ICT with trepidation. Its use requires them changing their work processes, which has costs implications for them, regardless of free technology, even if one considered only the training involved in the use of the technology, not to mention that they may not readily see the benefits that would accrue from such investments. One possible solution to this problem is further helping doctors defray at least some of the post-implementation costs of technology such as training, and maintenance costs. Change management initiatives, for example seminars for doctors would also help. By making them see the benefits of proposed technologies to their practice and to their patients, it would be much easier for them to embrace these technologies. Would it not make a difference in outlook to a particular technology if a doctor knew that implementing it would not only improve the quality of healthcare delivery to his or her patients, but would also reduce the chances of being sued, the technology ensuring evidence-based practice? What role does government have to play in minimizing malpractice suits, thus encouraging physicians to adopt health ICT, for example, the electronic health records systems (EHR)? Do companies also have a role to play in this concerted effort to promote healthcare ICT adoption by healthcare professionals? Should they not have their own set of incentive programs to encourage doctors to use healthcare ICT? It might all sound pampering, but would these efforts not benefit all concerned, the patients who receive the best care, the physician whose patient population increases, and does not have to worry about lawsuits, the payers that save substantially in health costs, and government that meets its commitments of ensuring comprehensive and qualitative health service provision at much reduced costs? To emphasize the importance of this subject, health costs would be the focus of the next State of the Union address by the US President George Bush on January 31, 2006₆. According to officials, issues in the President's speech include: raising the dollar amount allowed to accumulate in existing health savings accounts, in which accounts, people bear more of the responsibility for the costs of care, via tax-free money that they deposit into a dedicated account while purchasing a high-deductible policy to cover catastrophic expenses. Another is further tax breaks to help people who do not have employer-provided insurance coverage to buy their own. The government also wants to ensure more portability for health insurance when people switch jobs. The proposed tax breaks would certainly help many but some would argue that these measures amount to government shifting more of the healthcare burden on people that could least afford that sort of cost sharing. The third measure should compensate for some of the alleged defects of the Consolidated Omnibus Budget Reconciliation Act (COBRA) whose costs or those of any health insurance for that matter, most workers in between jobs often cannot pay, yet, COBRA was established essentially to provide, albeit temporarily, continuation coverage, for certain former employees, retirees, and their dependants at group rates. The reality however, is that coverage only occurs under certain circumstances, group health coverage for COBRA participants, usually costlier than for active employees, due to the fact that employers typically contribute a part of the premium for active employees but COBRA participants pay all of it themselves. The President s initiative some say, would increase the chances of the up to 14 million low-income workers in the US to benefit from the safety net of the public programs meant to provide health coverage for 56 million Americans that do not otherwise, due to the complex mix of exclusion criteria. According to officials, President Bush s proposals emanates from the conviction that controlling health care costs requires that choices be driven more directly by price-conscious, informed patient-shopper than by employers, insurers and others. This conviction is at the core of the current trend towards consumer-driven healthcare system, and expects consumer demands to drive the market into providing better and cheaper services. Critics on the other hand contend that focusing on providing tax advantages to persons for health spending pulls the healthy and well off out of conventional employer-based insurance, leaving behind the ill, and poor, in a system that is becoming more expensive and would be increasingly unavailable in the end. Whichever way one sees it, in the end, what matters is for persons to receive the healthcare services that they need. There is no doubt that individuals would continue to have even more say in their health affairs, including in the choices of providers that they make. Their ability to choose from providers would promote competition among providers, particularly in a health system that relies on private health insurance. This would no doubt enhance the quality of services provided, which is why employers and other payers should be interested in aligning with consumers to facilitate this sort of competition. Free-market forces would become operational sooner than later under these circumstances, with providers that want to survive let alone thrive implementing the necessary measures including appropriate healthcare ICT that would differentiate their services and improve their work processes, efficiency, and the quality of services that they provide. Competition would also drive prices down as providers would have to make pricing for their products and services competitive, and in keeping with those of their peers engaged in providing similar services, and under similar circumstances. These developments would not only make healthcare more affordable for individuals paying out of pocket, but also for companies purchasing services for their workers, essentially helping them contain health benefit costs. Insurers would also benefit from standardized practices backed by professional and government regulations, improved healthcare delivery and streamlined provider work processes, and other benefits that would accrue from implementing healthcare ICT. Low costs, timeliness, and accuracy of claims processing measure success and confer competitive advantage in the health insurance industry. Automating processes both by providers and insurers result in lower administrative costs and labor content vis-à-vis the number of members served. It also helps in the handling of actuarial data, crucial in facilitating the pricing of premiums, getting which right is perhaps the most important source of competitive edge in contemporary insurance business. The number of contracts insurance companies have is important, but more important for accurate pricing is accurate data on the number of clients they have, and their demographic characteristics, which information combined with regional, provincial, and local differences in the types of disorders and illnesses, and doctors practice modes, attitudes and behaviors becomes a veritable analytical tool. This highlights the need for both providers and insurers to implement the necessary secure and confidential ICT to facilitate data and information gathering and their transformation into actionable knowledge, and of information communication and sharing. ICT would also facilitate claims processing, and faster processing could help provide a more accurate idea costs and give insurers a head start on changing trends and patterns in the industry, making it possible for the insurer to increase or lower price as necessary. It would also help develop novel processes, such as real-time bill resolution, and others that would make the consumer s experience with the health insurance industry interactive, and rewarding. Indeed, the President s speech would expectedly have other proposals all, related to healthcare ICT implementation by both providers and payers. The first involves some means whereby people could obtain more information about the price of the care they receive and the performance of their doctors, which no doubt requires a variety of healthcare ICT, for example, the electronic health record (EHR) and evidence-based practice being in place. Another expected proposal is a move from paper-based medical records to more cost-effective, error-reducing electronic records. Also expected in the speech is a proposal to enable small businesses to pool the purchasing of health insurance coverage across state lines, a key opportunity for companies to reduce health benefit costs by not being stuck with insurers from which they are not obtaining value for their money. Indeed, Montana has passed a bill that encourages small businesses to unify resources to obtain health insurance, and the state provides tax incentives to businesses that offer insurance through the program. The US federal government also wants to put a cap on malpractice verdicts other than actual economic damages, about which proposal the President has been able to convince the House in three consecutive years, but not the Senate. Clearly, and there is no over-emphasizing the point, businesses also have a stake in encouraging the implementation of healthcare ICT by providers and insurers, because the more efficient the services these latter provide, the likelier higher the quality of the services they deliver. In the case of providers, would improve health, and reduce morbidities and mortalities, fostering a more productive work force, and reducing the overall health benefits costs. With regard insurers, ICT would facilitate claims processing, help identify and rectify claims errors, giving companies more accurate and timely records of the costs they incurred on their workers health services.

The 2006 report of the State Coverage Initiatives program, which in the US provides technical support to help states broaden health insurance coverage shows that states now spend more on Medicaid, healthcare for the poor, than they do on elementary and secondary education[7]. The report showed that states spent 21.9 percent of their budgets on Medicaid in fiscal year 2004, compared to 21.5% on elementary and secondary education, and 10.5% on higher education during the same period. The report also showed that many states have plans to expand health insurance coverage, albeit in different ways, Illinois, for example making insurance coverage available to all uninsured children, the premiums charged on an income-based sliding scale, Maryland, as noted above, mandating private-sector firms employing over 10,000 people to spend at least 8 percent of payroll on health care. Thus, states are trying to make a difference, in fact many blaming increasing Medicaid costs for the states on the continued decline in employer-sponsored health insurance. As previously noted, this might have informed the push by legislators for the sort of bill recently passed in Maryland, justifying which at least in part some would argue that Medicaid, in general after all, provides coverage for children who lost access to employer-sponsored coverage. COBRA and the expected proposal by President Bush mentioned earlier, expected to cover adults that are in-between jobs, not covered by Medicaid s employer-sponsored coverage, they would probably, add. Should companies not be seeking ways to reduce health benefit costs without creating an image problem for themselves? Few would disagree that companies need to reduce health benefit costs, just as governments and states are doing. However, the idea of reducing health benefits costs does not mean not providing health benefits. On the other hand, it means optimizing resources, ensuring judicious health spending, knowing where the company's health spending is going, obtaining value for money, ensuring the provision of qualitative health services to workers, and promoting disease prevention, among others. Healthcare ICT would help in achieving these objectives, hence the need to collaborate with healthcare providers, insurers, and governments to facilitate the implementation of healthcare ICT by all healthcare stakeholders, particularly doctors and nurses and other healthcare professionals. Paradoxically, companies would likely be better able to provide coverage for all their employers and continuing health care coverage to a certain extent even after they left the company and are in-between jobs, the duration of such coverage predetermined in an agreement. This agreement may include the worker making a token contribution to say, a healthcare account, to help defray such post-employment health costs. This is akin to the idea of the new Medicare savings accounts whereby individuals would have 1% of their earnings deducted from their paychecks and placed into an account, which they could later use to pay for long-term care, or other health services not covered by Medicare. Companies could also save costs preventing the duplicate billings some have complained about regarding certain physician practice types, for example, in the US, the so-called retainer practices, also termed, "concierge," or "boutique" practices. In these practices, patients pay a supplemental fee to their doctors for enhanced access and certain services, such as accompanied visits to specialists, which traditional primary care practices may not provide. Some claim that such retainer fees are duplicate billing if the doctors also accept insurance payments for services that they provide to the same patients[7]. Businesses also need to ensure that their workers registered in such practices do not receive unnecessary and improper services, which would constitute health care overuse, which some have accused such practices of, and which would increase benefits costs eventually[8]. There are important lessons from the past that employers could use in their efforts to control health benefits today. Some still blame the escalating costs of healthcare on Health Maintenance Organizations (HMOs) and the managed care movement of the 1980s, whose falling apart in the 1990s proponents of this point of view claim was partly due to employers turning HMOs against one another, and frequent plan switching, the later shuffling patients round providers. The effects of these problems, plus other issues such as complaints about limited options of doctors and hospitals, non-medical administrators determining health services provision, and long wait lists, among others compromised long-term healthcare objectives, and patients health. Ironically, these complaints led these health plans to loosen their grip over costs, which then started to soar, of course, employers, among those mostly bearing these costs. Employers would likely continue the current trend of knowing what they are spending money on regarding workers' health, particularly in the US where as many as 33 states are reportedly taking a cue from Maryland some, Washington, for example, having begun hearings on such legislation, and others, such as Georgia, and Ohio, planning to do so soon. These states apparently are unimpressed with Wal-Mart's protestations that such bills would not control rising healthcare costs, but rather would cost jobs and slow economic growth[8]. Many employers have already embraced the idea of "pay for performance", which many others consider the best solution for employers, not only to control health benefits costs, but also to improve the quality of the health services their workers receive. The scheme enables employers to demand excellence from insurers, who in turn would have to demand it from providers such as doctors and hospitals. Healthcare ICT would certainly be important to many of the quality measures required for this to happen, for insurers seek predictable costs and higher quality to continue to impress employers. Pay for performance programs designed for hospitals could, for example reward those that met insurers quality measures such as being "wired" with a chance to provide additional services, hence make more money than in the original contract. Insurers could keep back an aspect of the contract of those that remained "unwired" until they complied with implementing specified healthcare ICT, or other quality measures, for examples. They could have similar programs for physicians whereby "wired" practices and doctors that use healthcare ICT receive bonus payments, or other tangible compensations. Indeed, ICT becomes crucial even in the evaluation of outcomes of intervention, on which performance rests, for example, that provided by evidence-based interventions. There would be need for companies and insurers to keep abreast of medical knowledge in order to know which interventions work and which do not, as that is perhaps the best way to specify those they would reward. Even those that seem obvious, for example, the use of aspiring in patients presenting with chest pain in the ER as an important measure in reducing mortality from heart attacks, would require continual evaluation of research evidence to determine under what circumstances the practice yields better outcomes or if new knowledge suggests it really does not. In the latter case, for example, the practice should cease prompting rewards. Would pay-for-performance reduce healthcare costs? Clearly, by improving the quality of care, it would reduce physician visits, morbidities, hospitalization rates, medications costs, costs of laboratory investigations, and the like, thus overall health costs, one reason it makes sense not just for all health insurers, public or private, to embrace it, but also employers. Additionally, some of the savings derivable from the program could go into developing newer health insurance programs, for the millions, in the US, for example, who currently lack health insurance, for example, children, which some estimates put at almost nine million, and seniors. A recent Commonwealth Fund survey in the US, for example, showed that 60% of workers ages 50 to 64 and their spouses have at least one chronic medical problem, placing them at greater risk of incurring high medical costs than younger adults, high blood pressure, arthritis, and high cholesterol, the commonest problems. A fifth of them is not insured or had not been at least once, since turning 50 years old10. Would current proposals to expand health coverage of older adults by providing tax credits to low-income individuals to purchase health insurance help? Should employers lend a hand? The survey also showed that 55% of older adults with coverage on the individual market spend $3,600 or more yearly on premiums, compared to just 16% with employer coverage. Older adults with individual coverage not just pay higher premiums, 48% of them have per-person annual deductibles of $1,000 or higher, compared to just 8% of those with employer coverage, according to this survey. Furthermore, 38% of uninsured older adults and 37% of those with individual market coverage spend $1,000 or more yearly on out-of-pocket health care costs, including prescription drugs, compared with 21%, with employer coverage, and those in low- and moderate-income working households, a larger percentage of their of their income on out-of-pocket costs than those in higher-income households. Is mandating employers to increase healthcare benefits the solution to such problems or is it tax credit proposal? Developed countries with an aging population cannot afford to ignore these problems, which essentially would be taking lesser rather than better care of their seniors population, individuals that have contributed, and in some cases, continue to add significantly to societal progress, quite apart from their rights to qualitative and comprehensive healthcare like everyone else.

The health insurance conundrum clearly cuts across age groups, although not restricted to age groupings. Strictly speaking, employers could argue that it is the business of government and not theirs to worry about catering for the health of a country, that they are concerned with their workers and no one else. However, their workers have dependants that they also must worry about, and some are young, others old, with implications for health bills. Keeping a close eye on these bills is another important measure companies need to take to control and contain them, for example to detect wrong or overcharged bills, which they or their insurance firms, might not detect, which also makes the need for appropriate ICT for identifying such problems, necessary. Figures published for the 2002-2003 fiscal year for the UK for example showed continuing overcharges to its National Health Service (NHS) for surgeries contracted to private health providers11. The NHS reference cost for a coronary bypass surgery was £6320 or $11 280, but 1600 of them done on NHS patients by private contractors 2003, cost on the average, £ 12060, or 91% more. Each hip replacement NHS staff performed, cost an average £ 4660, compared to £ 6848 for private hip replacements, NHS officials estimating total markup at about 40%. The NHS might have justified these expenses as necessary to cut down wait lists, particularly in the short term, but companies may have to scrutinize such figures, particularly in relation to other performance and quality measures to justify them, or seek health services elsewhere. That the report also showed that it cost the NHS about £ 100m to purchase acute treatment services from the private sector, when it would cost about £ 70m, provided by NHS staff, also tells how much companies could save depending on which healthcare organizations, even within the private sector, their workers use. The point is not dumping healthcare providers or plans that use them just because their services are expensive, but that the pricing of services should be competitive, for similar services, delivered at equivalent quality standards, under identical geo-economic circumstances. Companies, for example, should also not have to bear the economic costs of spot services purchasing or of multiplicity of purchases for small work volumes, both of which swell health costs, and require a clear statement of this position to insurers, embodied in the original contractual agreements. Government, with its powerful purchaser advantage, could drive down costs, in the long term, by tweaking its medical education, and physician recruitment, and retention policies, for examples. Perhaps, they could therefore keep buying private health services until prices fall, but companies cannot afford such luxury, as their here-and-now position is crucial to their very survival, and equally critical for them to recognize their lack of the sort of lead that government has in this regard. They need therefore to track their money, although that is not to say that they would not benefit from government efforts in the long term to drive fees down. Much as general practice fundholding does in the UK, managed care in the US has strove to provide doctors an incentive to balance the needs of each patient with the cost of care, although there has been much criticism regarding managed care stifling doctors', curtailing consumer choices, and the like. However, it seems that the old debate of the 1990s in the US, regarding the merits or otherwise of regulating the market to promote competition among plans based on cost and quality rather than being able to select the healthiest clients has crept back, albeit surreptitiously into the zeitgeist. This is not surprising though, considering that many of the concerns regarding managed care persist. With research evidence from Kaiser Permanente group practice for example giving managed care a strong showing on both patient and doctor satisfaction, the former in particularly regarding cost, coverage, and the use of healthcare ICT to improve the quality of care, the new face of managed care is stressing the need for outcomes to show quality of care. Little wonder that some experts recommend that companies shun the fee-for-service model of care, which some claim encourage doctors to provide more services than necessary, and patients to overuse health services, not to mention the heightened risk of iatrogenic harm, all eventually contributing to soaring health costs and as some contend, even to inflation by providing the economy minimal incentives. On the other hand, should companies subscribe to the use of contracts with selected physicians and hospitals, which should presumably provide comprehensive health care services to members for a monthly premium, the typical managed care arrangement? Should companies and insurers prepay for services or pay for performance? There is no doubt in the wisdom of consumers choosing their physicians but what should determine these choices, should it be the physician their friend visited or liked, or should they have sufficient factual information on the expertise of the physician and the quality of services of his or her health organization? What implications does this freedom of choice have for the bottom line of companies? For example, is it ok for a company to switch health plans willy-nilly, or should they have consideration for their workers for example, a pregnant female worker who would not have to switch obstetrician in the middle of her pregnancy? How is healthcare ICT helping, and could help even more, to remove the information asymmetry that partly diminishes consumers abilities to make rational choices regarding physicians and treatment options? How could workers having such abilities help companies reduce health benefit costs, and obviate the need for them to be overly involved in their workers choices of healthcare providers after all? Could healthcare ICT implementation by healthcare providers that provide relevant, current, and timely healthcare information to their workers, including those that promote health and help prevent diseases, not to mention, those that improve the quality of service delivery not ultimately help companies reduce health benefit costs? Should companies therefore not be encouraging health plans, and providers to implement such ICT, incrementally if not radically? The provision of coverage for low-income people, the elderly, and children, ensuring continuity of coverage, and rectifying inequities in health services provision remain urgent problems confronting health financing in many countries, problems that many believe that controlling and containing health costs via incentives, and regulated private sector competition would solve, at least substantially. The private employer has a major role in this regard. Official figures revealed that 61% of Americans received health insurance via employers in the US in 1996, but the estimates included workers, primarily government-sponsored for example on Medicare, those for who their employers just set insurance up but the workers paid the premiums, and government workers taxpayers paid their private coverage. A research study published in the January 14, 1999 volume of the New England Journal of Medicine, however showed that in 1996, only 43.1% of the population depended primarily on health insurance that private sector employers paid for, 34.2%, on publicly funded insurance, 7.1% bought their own coverage, and 15.6% were uninsured12. These figures, which some say for private companies have improved, but others believe have actually fallen, led some to clamor for more employer participation in health insurance, reflecting in such new legislative measures as Maryland's "Fair Share Health Care Fund" bill, which some have dubbed the "Wal-Mart Bill". That the bill gives companies the option to pay into the state's insurance program for the poor underscores certain ethical dimensions to business operations that some would find difficult to swallow. Nonetheless, there are others for who the idea of "health for all" implies profound social responsibility, and yet, others would wonder to what extent companies should pay for the health services of those not on their payroll, or other social services, for that matter. There are also those that would ask what the implications of forcing companies to make those contributions, as opposed using some other subtle means to appeal to their social conscience, for example, would portend for the health of a free market economy. Debates on these questions have now moved beyond academic or other circles, and are before the law courts. The issues further stress the need for employers to explore ways to contain health benefits costs, simultaneously fulfilling their responsibilities to their employees. There is certainly no "silver bullet" for fixing health-financing problems, but with all stakeholders relentlessly examining ways by which they could collaborate in tackling them, appropriate solutions would likely emerge in tandem.

References

1. Katzmarzyk PT, and Mason C, Prevalence of class I, II and III obesity in Canada *CMAJ* •January 17, 2006; 174 (2)

2. Rhodes, A.E., Bethell, J., & Bondy, SJ. Suicidality, Depression, and Mental Health Service Use in Canada. *Can J Psychiatry*, Vol. 51, No 1, January 2006. Pp35-41

3. Alberta: More money for mental health. *National Review of Medicine,* January 15, 2006 p19

4. Goeree, R., Farahati, F., Burke, N., et al. The Economic Burden of Schizophrenia in Canada in 2004 *Curr Med Res Opin*. 2005; 21(12):2017-2028.

5. Goeree R, O'Brien BJ, Goering P, et al. The economic burden of schizophrenia in Canada. *Can J Psychiatry* 1999; 44:464-72

6. Available at: http://www.newsday.com/news/politics/wire/sns-ap-bush-state-of-union,0,6066546.story?coll=sns-ap-politics-headlines
Accessed on January 19, 2006.

7. Alert warns of Medicare conflict for concierge practices. *American MedicalNews*. April 19, 2004:1, 2.

8. Donohue M. Luxury primary care, academic medical centers, and the erosion of science and professional ethics. *J Gen Intern Med*. 2004; 19 90⁻4.

9. Available at:
http://www.kaisernetwork.org/daily_reports/rep_index.cfm?DR_ID=34900
Accessed on: January 20, 2006

10. Available at:

http://www.cmwf.org/usr_doc/884_Collins_hlt_coverage_aging_baby_boomers.pdf,
Accessed on:

11. Available at: http://bmj.bmjjournals.com/cgi/content/full/328/7449/1158-e
Accessed on; January 12, 2006.

12. Carrasquillo, O, Himmelstein, D.U, Woolhandler, S, and Bor, D.H. A Reappraisal of
Private Employers role in Providing Health Insurance. NEJM, V. 340: 109-114, Jan 14,
1999, No. 2

ICT and the Future of Hospitals

Prosthetic orthopedics has entered a new, virtual reality, phase, courtesy of the IST-funded MULTISENSE project. Using combined virtual reality, force-feedback systems, tissue profiling, and stereoscopic vision to create virtual patients that mimic the tissue of real patients, surgeons can now perform a hip-replacement operation on a virtual copy of their real patient, and even obtain a post-surgery read-out on the chances of the operation's success. Unlike in the past when they sometimes did not know if and why an implant failed, surgeons would have an idea if an implant in a certain patient would succeed or fail. The technology of the MULTISENSE system is the Muscular Modeling tool, a semi-automatic modeling function that reconstructs someone's muscle tissue virtually from data obtained from CT scans. Prior to now, medical systems existed that could only replicate specific disorders such as myocarditis, for teaching purposes, but it is now possible to adapt the MULTISENSE system to model the tissue of specific individuals, and obtain a fairly precise assessment of the outcome of the planned virtual surgery. The Muscle Modeling system is an application of medical haptics, a superior form of the haptic, or force-feedback, system employed in the joysticks of games consoles. This technology creates the force and resistance of real tissue, enabling the surgeon to experience the sensation of real surgery when they make an incision, an experience heightened by the system being voice controllable with simple commands, for example the system adjusting the feel more precisely to a surgeon saying he is lifting the skin. The devices also have a stereoscopic viewing system that enables the surgeon to see, and feel, the surgery during the planning phase. The system appears promising particularly in the developed world with an increasingly aging population, as it cuts down the rates of implant failures hence the overall healthcare costs of patients who need hip implants. The MULTISENSE currently focuses on planning surgeries but would soon be able to work in Computer-Aided Surgery, essentially also assisting in the surgical operations. This is just one example of the increasingly sophisticated ICT deployed in clinical practice, some of which would have direct bearing on the future practice of Medicine, for example, enabling the conduct of some surgical procedures remotely, and safely, in a non-hospital facility, even right at the patient's home, with physician assistants or community nurses in attendance, saving treatment costs. Computer-aided detection (CAD) is also making significant differences to radiological practice. The results of a large multicenter study presented at the 2005 annual meeting of the radiological Society of North America, indicated comparability of the sensitivity and false positive rates of virtual colonoscopy with CAD to conventional colonoscopy for diagnosing precancerous polyps. This means that radiologists no longer have to worry about errors they are prone to making reading the numerous images virtual colonoscopy alone produces, often 600 to 1,000 per patient. In other words, CAD would enable them to read virtual colonoscopy more accurately, and under less pressure. It would also make it easier for them to encourage their patients to undergo virtual colonoscopy. This is because unlike conventional colonoscopy, which utilizes an optical scope, with virtual colonoscopy, a computer reconstructs X-rays of the colon's interior surface in two or three dimensions, the result, much reduced complications rates, and examination and recovery periods, and coupled with becoming less costly for patients, would likely attract more people, hence increasing its prospects for screening populations. Furthermore, because the technology is able to detect polyps 1cm or more, in size, the range at which they could more likely become or already are cancerous, and when surgical removal is preferred, the technology could save many lives, the procedures involved in colonoscopy with CAD examination readily conducted in non-hospital health centers.

Guided laser technology is also making it possible to perform surgery for the treatment of liver tumors on an outpatient basis. Recent large, long-term research studies have shown that the hardly invasive procedure of laser ablation of liver tumors with Magnetic Resonance (MR) guidance is just as effective as traditional open surgery. Laser ablation, otherwise known as laser-induced thermotherapy (LITT) requires only local anesthesia, is also readily repeatable, an asset in the treatment of cancers that have started to metastasize or spread, in treating new growths hence saving the patient the trouble of undergoing repeated open surgeries, has significantly fewer morbidities and complications, and is cost-effective. Digital tomosynthesis, a 3-D breast imaging technique, surpassed, was equivalent to, and inferior to mammography, 35%, 54%, and 12% of the time respectively, according to recent reports by a research team at Dartmouth Hitchcock Medical Center and School in Lebanon, N.H. led by Dr Steven

Poplack. By taking multiple X-rays of each breast from a variety of angles, unlike the two of conventional mammography, and it is possible to manipulate and display the data in many different ways, the chances of overlying tissue mistaken for or concealing minute lesions becoming less likely, the characteristics of a suspicious much better evident. With the potential for a 40% decrease in screening mammography recall rates, this technique, would save time, costs, and women a lot of worry, and mobilized, may in future replace mammography as the preferred breast cancer-screening tool. Still on imaging, researchers at the Aachen University Hospital in Germany recently published the results of their studies of a new procedure for the imaging of coronary veins that is less invasive and has fewer complications, in the American Journal of Roentgenology. According to the researchers, this new procedure termed, ECG-gated cardiac modified discrete cosine transform, or MDCT, angiography improves the quality of diagnosis and treatment for persons undergoing heart surgery, particularly on the coronary veins. The new procedure facilitates planning for surgeries on the coronary veins by enabling detailed knowledge of the patient's anatomy, which is important for the surgery's success as the coronary veins are variable in number, caliber, and course, with each person. It is likely that in the near future, MDCT angiography would prove to be more widely use than invasive conventional coronary angiography, to evaluate the coronary veins prior to pacemaker lead placement, and sundry procedures. Would these and other cutting-edge ICT, lead to the emergence of new, more cost-effective models of healthcare delivery, for example, in ubiquitous but less costly healthcare facilities, improving accessibility to healthcare professionals via virtual consultation and treatment, hence reducing wait times, fostering equity, and improving the quality of service delivery? What implications would this have for service outsourcing between private healthcare providers and between them and the public health system? Would this outsourcing even be cross-national? What changes in legal, regulatory, and other instruments would each country have to put in place to address the various ethical, medico-legal, and other issues that would inevitably arise with such outsourcing arrangements? What role would ICT play in all these? With increasing healthcare costs, it seems rational that countries are examining options for delivering qualitative healthcare to their citizens more cost-effectively. In Canada, provincial governments are responsible for healthcare delivery. Some of them are already signaling their intentions to move their health policies and programs in new directions. Premier Ralph Klein of Alberta, for example has outlined plans for a "third way" of healthcare for the province[1], which according to the Premier, would follow neither the American system nor the purely Canadian version of health care but that respects the Canada Health Act. The Premier, who announced the plan on July 12, 2005, intends to draw on the experiences and best ideas from other health care systems in Canada and other countries stressing the need to control and contain skyrocketing healthcare costs, while ensuring that someone's ability to pay will never determine access health care in the province. The Premier, who affirmed his intention to implement key recommendations of the Mazankowski Report on healthcare reform, also noted that by January 2008, every patient would have an electronic health file, available to all health professionals across the province, and plans to form committees to review new and emerging health services for possible public funding. Children's education, including incorporating wellness into the curriculum, changes to the delivery of mental health services, particularly increasing access to services, and the establishment of a new mental health innovation fund to encourage and fund local initiatives to improve services for people with mental illnesses, including youth mental health services, are also prominent on the Premier's agenda.

According to the US National Center for Health Statistics records for 2000, there were over 1 billion visits to doctors offices and hospital outpatient departments and the figures have been rising ever since. Total healthcare spending in ambulatory care settings including solo physician settings, group practices, and hospital outpatient units, equals or surpasses that in acute care such as inpatient medical and surgical units, and critical care units, yet health ICT investments in the former remains small compared to the latter. The US ambulatory EMR market increased from $0.8 billion to $1.2 billion at a yearly rate of 22% between 2003 and 2005, which contrasts with the total healthcare ICT market for acute care in the same period from $39 billion to $45 billion, at a yearly growth rate of only 7%. For just hospital-based clinical information technology, a recent research from Kalorama Information published in September 2005 estimated the U.S. market at $25 billion by 2009. What really then is the fate of the hospital and what role would ICT play in its unfolding evolution? The answer to this question is multi-dimensional, hinged on how a variety of factors such as treatment costs, healthcare financing arrangements, benefit plans, health indicators, demographics, the progress of medical knowledge, health policies and reforms, and prevalence patterns of diseases, among others, play out within a technology substrate. Let us illustrate treatment costs with leg ulcers, a relatively common medical problem, associated with venous vascular diseases, with such contributory factors as obesity, diabetes, trauma, arterial disease, immobility, vasculitis, and cancers. Leg ulcers not only create problems for patients, considering their prevalence, particularly in aging populations, enormous drain on scarce health services resources[2], the annual cost of venous leg ulceration alone to the UK National Health Service (NHS) estimated at $720 million[2], most of it, spent on community nursing services[3]. It seems anachronistic that these conditions, best managed in the hospital with continuous leg elevation, end up managed otherwise, high hospital costs, shortage of hospital beds, and the quest for the often-elderly population concerned for independence and quality of life, some of the reasons why[2]. The NHS continues on efforts to improve the cost-effectiveness of outpatient and community-based care for these seniors and others with leg ulcers, including on programs to encourage and maintain mobility and to avoid the complications of bed rest as the ulcers usually recurred with the patient s leg in dependency positions, and closely supervised use of compression bandaging. These and other measures ultimately facilitate healing and are more cost-effective than hospitalization, making the latter even less likely for individuals with leg ulcers in future. Would other countries adopt this approach to managing leg ulcers? How many other diseases do cost drive their management? How could such cost considerations determine the future of hospitals? If indeed, hospitals as we know them are moribund, what role does ICT have in facilitating the smooth operations of the healthcare delivery models that evolve, particularly in ensuring their seamless collaboration and coordination? There are indeed, signs of changing times regarding the financial arrangements of health services provision, most notably in Canada with the recent Supreme Court decision in Quebec essentially giving legal backing to private health services operations in the province. On December 27, 2005, in British Columbia, Macquarie Bank Ltd., Australia's largest investment bank, announced its acquisition of an 81-per-cent stake in two British Columbia health-care projects worth C$450 million, from ABN Amro Holding NV, the latter, the largest Dutch lender, holding the remaining stake in the projects. The Sydney-based Macquarie Bank, which oversees funds that control more than A$112 billion ($81 billion US) of assets in the U.S., South Korea, U.K., Canada, and other countries, also indicated that it may transfer the Abbotsford Regional Hospital and Cancer Centre and the Academic Ambulatory Care Centre projects into investment funds that it will administer[4]. The electorate in California passed Proposition 63, the Mental Health Services Act (MHSA), in the 2004 California election, mandating a 1 percent increase in individual income taxes for Californians earning more than $1 million annually. Distribution of the revenues generated from the tax increase, projected to be an average of $700 million per year to the county mental health departments would fund the transformation of public mental health service systems statewide, in several phases, which would coincide with the introduction of MSHA's primary components. These components are Education and Training; Capital Facilities and Technology; Prevention and Early Intervention; and Community Services and Supports (CSS), the latter, which alone constitutes more than half of the expected yearly MHSA funding, the first that counties would implement. Yolo County, for example, has received over $5.6 million for homegrown, Community Services and Supports programs over the next three fiscal years, about $1.8 million per year [5, 6]. The county also received $124,000 to disburse for the MHSA community planning process, which commenced in March 2005. Yolo county's proposed programs involved the active participation of hundreds of Yolo County stakeholders, including members of the Local Mental Health Board, in its planning process. Participants attended several evening meetings, perused numerous documents, formed a Community Planning Council and five subcommittees, namely, Children, Transition-Age Youth, Adult, Older Adult, and Forensics, and wrote and rewrote draft program plans. They also collaborated with the Alcohol and Drugs Mental Health Services (ADMHS) Management Team and the MHSA Coordinator to develop the proposed Community Services and Supports three-Year Program and Expenditure Plan. The Plan would have public hearings and accept written comments on it by interested county citizens in January 2006, before funding, and then program implementation proceed. Would other US states adopt the new California model of funding and programming mental health services? What implications does this model have for the future of psychiatric hospitals? How much role would ICT play in the achievement of the objectives of this new mental health services model? Should software and ICT firms be interested in developments such as this in the health industry? How might this help them in strategizing? [6]

Speaking at the 2005 Canadian Psychiatric Association (CPA) annual conference, Senator (Dr.) Wilbert Keon, Vice-chair of the Senate Standing Committee on Social Affairs, Science, and Technology, expected to deliver its report on the state of mental health in Canada early in 2006, urged psychiatrists to come up with new approaches of making integrated community care available to all Canadians[7]. The Senator specifically asked the psychiatrists, gathered in Vancouver in November to help build an effective community-based primary care system, which would improve mental health care delivery. He also hinted at the recommendations in the imminent report, one key treatment approach being a qualitative, multidisciplinary, and integrated patient-centered, recovery-focused, system customized to meet individual needs, with emphasis on seamlessly integrating and coordinating the activities of various services and mental health resources, which underscore the important role ICT, would play in achieving this goal. Senator Keon stressed the need to base mental health on a primary care model via community clinics, and for private financing of mental health services, which would foster competition, in turn service improvement, and facilitate the provision of mental health services to all Canadians. Noting that Canada spends about 10% of its gross domestic product (GDP) on health, and with that percentage rising, and most Canadians quite concerned about increasing health spending by the government, yet demanding improved and more services, the Senator stressed the need for collaboration between government and the health insurance industry in order to achieve both goals simultaneously. Senator Keon recommended the single payer system whereby individuals have the option to choose between public and private health services, on account of the efficiency and quality of their services, after delivery, as the best healthcare model for Canada. With a service-based, rather than the current global budget, funding model and healthcare providers being paid and agreed fee for services rendered, after delivery, the Senator noted that this model would ensure competition for patient s on the basis of price and quality, and that people are paid for what they do regardless of who provides the service. What are the implications for hospitals of the recommendations of Senator Keon s committee? To be sure, no government is likely to close down hospitals en masse as occurred in the 1960s and 1970s, including the ill-fated policy of deinstitutionalization of the mentally ill, without adequate provision of community services and resources for the masses of patients unceremoniously discharged from the psychiatric hospitals, an example of a well-intentioned but poorly implemented policy. The US Community Mental Health Centers Construction Act of October 31, 1963 meant well, but the country needed 2000-community mental health centers built by 1980, although just about 482 received Federal construction funds from 1963 to 1980, and the program actually metamorphosed into the Alcohol, Drug Abuse, and Mental Health block grant program in 1981 and into oblivion thereafter. There were similar mass closures of hospitals in Canada and other countries during the same period with negative consequences for health services provision that has lingered until today in certain respects. It would therefore be most unlikely for anyone to advocate a return to that era. Nonetheless the preceding no doubt shows the precariousness of the entity we call the hospital, as we know it today. The seemingly unstoppable wave of free market incursion into health care delivery even in countries with strong social welfare credentials suggest that healthcare is yet emerging into another era, one in which technologies and other forces are redefining the place of the traditional hospital in contemporary health services delivery. Rural hospitals for example, are quite vulnerable to competitive pressures due to being small, often with outmoded infrastructure, and lacking in strategic opportunities, hence many close down. Such rural hospitals cannot survive in today's highly competitive healthcare market prosecuting a price war with the larger hospitals, particularly because they are unlikely to have as much financial resources as the latter. However, rural hospitals do not have to close down. They simply need to become a bit more creative and device means by which to compete more effectively within their restricted budget for example via differentiation, defining and vigorously pursuing a profitable market niche, armed with an appropriate service configuration. Such a niche is a market segment maybe in a geographical, or even a more culture-based catchment area, with enough clients that are willing to purchase their services, and with enough entry barriers to minimize competition. Research has shown that among other factors, hospitals, including those in rural areas that offer more high-tech services than the market average are at a lower risk of closure than their competition in the same market area. It is likely therefore that hospitals would experience more pressure that could result in closure the less they are "wired", hence most probably less competitive, which would hold, even for a government hospital, in an environment in which it has to compete cost-effectively, for example, with private healthcare providers in say a single payer health financing system. Indeed, government might find it expedient economically and otherwise to replace some traditional hospitals with more flexible horizontally managed community health centers, but retain them under different circumstances, and in other locations. They may also prefer to buy certain services, for example, long-term neuro-rehabilitation services for the brain injured or services for the mentally retarded or mental health services for young offenders, from private healthcare providers to cover certain catchment areas rather than establish those services only to run into difficulties either staffing them, or managing them cost-effectively. Viewed from another angle, such liaison would likely stimulate interest by healthcare providers in developing innovative services for identified market niches in the country. This would create jobs, perhaps where they were hitherto lacking, fostering family stability and social cohesion as bread winners no longer have to venture away from home in search of employment, and facilitating the country's overall economic growth. Furthermore, by purchasing services from the best provider at the best price, government would be encouraging healthy competition among service providers while ensuring that the public receives the highest quality of needed health services. It would also be able to keep health spending in check, with more resources available to focus on the other health services it still provides, and indeed, for other social and other services it needs to provide. Developments within the public health services would therefore be influencing the future direction of today's government-owned hospitals, as services become more decentralized in order to spread them further away from their usual locations in the cities and larger towns, so that more citizens have ready access to healthcare services. However, the consequences of these developments would spill over to the private health sector, with investors and private healthcare providers increasingly providing specialized services, with resultant changes in the infrastructure and management of private hospitals, some of these services essentially outpatient-based, others ambulatory, and some even home-based. There is likely to be increasing collaboration between different specialist service providers, under some sort of business arrangement best suited to the partners, with service facilities emerging that not only look very different from today's hospitals, but also function differently, due in the main to very profound technology involvement. There is no doubt about the complexity of the factors that would determine the fate of the hospital, but they would in the end, be intimately interwoven, and bear important relevancies to the particular country in question.

Managed care in the US, for example, reduced the yearly increases in healthcare costs from 18% to 4%, but the increases have bounced back into double digits. This has prompted some experts to suggest the solution being to revisit a health financing model termed, prepaid group practice (PGP), an integrated entity that includes both a healthcare delivery system comprising doctors, laboratories, clinics, and hospitals, and an insurance function compromising financing arrangements, benefit plans, marketing, and customer service systems under one roof 8 . The model has essentially experts in various specialties, providing comprehensive services to a patient population that enrolled willingly, prepayment being by enrolling, and prepared to be accountable for the costs and quality of the services they provide. PGP plan members pay premiums periodically to the plan, and receive the health services the plan provides, as and when needed, with no further charges, and many PGPs have arrangements with Medicare to receive direct payments for services they provide covered by Part B (SMI). The US spends about US$6500 on healthcare per person annually, roughly US$1.5 trillion per year, yet has about 44 million uninsured individuals. It is therefore, not surprising that many believe that its health system needs radical reforms, including closing the gap between health care finance and health care organization and quality, for which some experts suggest PGP. Implementing an improved PGP model would necessitate structural changes in healthcare delivery in the country, including modifying our current concepts of the hospital and of its functions. Protagonists of this model, including Alain Enthoven, the respected, emeritus Marriner S. Eccles Professor of Public and Private Management at Stanford University, and the originator of a health care strategy termed managed competition, predicate its potential on being able to customize treatment to meet the individual patient s needs, cost-effectively because of PGPs acquaintance with their patient population and its peculiarities. Furthermore, they contend that doctors attracted to such physician groups are likely to be less conventional, making it easier for them to imbibe a culture of excellence, including strict adherence to evidence-based practice, and to pursue high quality service delivery. Such groups would also likely invest substantially in appropriate healthcare ICT, including technologies that facilitate patient education and support, as integral and critical contributors to their achievement of excellence. They would also likely appreciate the importance of apposite recompense for services provided, hence have the right reward system in place, and establish the necessary partnerships with healthcare services for examples, hospitals, and health plans, to ensure that there is continuity of service provision to their clients, even if they had to receive the services elsewhere. Some would ask why recommend managed care when it had failed so miserably. Yet, some argue that the "true nature" of the "consumer-driven" healthcare delivery system opponents of managed care flock to, is becoming increasingly evident, as beneath its mantle lay a progressive depletion of enrollees healthcare coverage9. However, today's managed-care market, based on competing health plans of provider networks of healthcare coverage for most employed persons, and over 50% of those on Medicaid continues to increase healthcare costs. The argument by some that the flaw was in its execution and not the idea regardless there is strong fervor for a health system in the US that would contain and curtail health costs yet provide healthcare coverage for all its citizens. Perhaps PGP would help, but it has its own problems, some doctors feeling too restricted by evidence-based practice, which they criticize as being fluid depending on the rate of change to current "evidence", among others, and some unable to overcome their confessed-to technophobia. Another important likely hindrance to PGP implementation is the reluctance of some group sponsors and insurers to accept legal accountability of healthcare quality hence tendency to shun health care processes, and structural matters. The 2004 U.S. Supreme Court ruling in *Aetna* v. *Davila* that prohibited health plan members the Employee Retirement Income Security Act sponsors to hold health insurers and plan administrators accountable for likely consequences of slack medical conduct linked with the coverage, exemplifies this fear of legal liability. This ruling, which essentially extricates healthcare financing from quality, would likely create major problems for implementing a prepayment system. These problems notwithstanding, proponents of PGP could seek succor in the remarkable successes of some of the predecessors of prepaid group practices. In the early days, when they were termed "lodge medicine,10" some of the workplace associations, fraternal societies and immigrant groups, and mutual benefits societies that "contracted" with doctors for healthcare provision to their members even built their own hospitals, San Francisco s

French Hospital, now owned by Kaiser Permanente, being one of such hospitals. It is a relic of a facility the Société Française de Bienfaisance Mutuelle, built in 1852 to provide prepaid care for French immigrants[11]. However, would modern day group practices be doing the exact opposite, redefining the concept of the hospital, operating in high-tech facilities tailor-made to deliver specific services and located in strategic market niches? Group practices, on the other hand, have transitioned historically, from one form to another, the Mayo Clinic, the prototypical group practice, for example, used to be a solo practice way back in 1866[12]. Kaiser Permanente, and Mayo Clinic, representing the "prepaid contract medicine" and the "group practice" origins of the two aspects of PGP respectively have been both remarkably successful health service organizations, the former, easily the largest PGP in the US to date[s] prepaid group practice the solution for an equitable and accessible, yet cost-effective health system? Indeed, the US Congress has enacted legislation authorizing a mortgage insurance program to make funds available on reasonable terms to facilitate the construction of medical, optometric, dental, osteopathic, and podiatric group practice facilities, apparently in recognition of the need for these services that often require substantial financial outlay. Advocates of the group practice model argue that it optimizes the use of scarce professional resources, and expensive, often-multispecialty health care facilities and high-tech equipment. They stress that group practices can be especially advantageous to small communities, rural areas, where they could have branches, and low-income urban areas where adequate and comprehensive health services may be lacking, and that group practices would significantly reduce expensive hospitalization costs, particularly when combined with an inclusive prepayment plan. The new, improved PGP may help reduce healthcare costs in the US and may be the way to go, but the almost a dozen national health insurance carriers in the US seem to be waxing stronger. Analysts expect the new US Medicare Part D prescription-drug benefit to be a key driver of the health-insurance sector in 2006. With enrollment of many news members into health plans anticipated, via health maintenance organizations (HMOs), and preferred provider organizations (PPOs), and the (Medicare Part D plan, and with health plans expected to form strategic alliances in this highly competitive marketplace, this may really be the case. A ready example of such alliances is that between United Health Group and American Association of Retired Persons, the latter, seniors trust. Analysts also expect WellPoint, strong in the

American Midwest, to collaborate with WellChoice in 2006. Medicare's new program will take effect on Jan. 1, 2006, also revealing a new plan, the Medicare PPO, which major health-insurance players also highly anticipate and would therefore be very likely highly competitive. This new plan offers seniors across the country, whether in urban or rural areas, access to the plans, previously only feasible economically, hence restricted to urban areas. The managed-care industry therefore, still thrives in the US, and becoming even more privatized, with mergers and acquisitions creating managed-care behemoths, for example the United Health Group and PacifiCare merger in December 2005, in a $9.2 billion deal experts deem the second-largest buyout in the history of the managed-care industry. With managed-care plans expected to grow their Medicare Advantage business by over a million members, or 17 percent, in 2006, and to 24 percent three years later, the merger trend will unlikely ease with Aetna actually tipped to embark on an acquisition binge, probably swooping Humana and Coventry Health Plan, in 2006. How would these mergers influence the future of hospitals? Indeed, this trend, some argue, would only benefit health plans, whose administrative costs among others would fall drastically. They also contend that consumers and employers seeking health plans for their employees, in local and regional markets would have increasingly fewer options. Many that advocate PGP would point to this problem as one of the reasons the think that PGP offers better hope for Americans to receive comprehensive, equitable, high-tech, and affordable healthcare. With quality a sine qua non for prepayment, the commitment to process improvement and the delivery of healthcare services in the most appropriate structural milieu would be mandatory, but cost-effective for PGPs. Default on contracts could result in litigation. Could such enforced quality service provision occur with other health plans, particularly the implementation of appropriate healthcare ICT? How would the prevailing, anticipated, and suggested scenarios in the American health insurance industry influence the future structure and function of the hospital? If, indeed, healthcare ICT has an underlying but significant role to play in the delivery of qualitative healthcare, should software and ICT firms not have a stake in how the dynamics between the various factors that would determine what the structure and function, and the geographic spread of future hospitals play out? Should they, for example, not be supporting, if not actually promoting the adoption of quality as an essential component of future healthcare delivery? Would that therefore not imply taking reasonable measures such as offering incentives to healthcare providers to implement ICT and encouraging consumers and payers to insist on minimal healthcare ICT standards where they would receive health services? What would a software or ICT firm lose taking measures whose costs would ultimately pale in significance relative to the benefits it would derive from soaring sales in an expanded market? Private health insurance supplements Canada's Medicare, which might change with more extensive private health insurance involvement in the country's healthcare delivery if a parallel private health system emerged in the country, in which case, the impact of healthcare ICT on the future direction of the hospital would even be significantly more. This would be so because of the necessary reorientation of healthcare providers that some other key healthcare drivers such as demographics and health indicators would demand.

The developed world, including Canada is an aging population. Aging has associated health problems, the changing approaches to addressing which would bear significantly on the future of hospitals in the country. Certain diseases are more prevalent in the older age groups, for example Alzheimer's disease and the dementias, and create management challenges both for the relatives of the individuals that suffer from these conditions, and for healthcare providers. Healthcare ICT certainly helps with meeting these management challenges, particularly as many of the conditions are amenable to domiciliary management, an approach increasingly gaining favor among health policy makers, and which would influence where, and what types of health facilities they build, or scrap and replace with more appropriate health facility, based on the characteristics of the population served. Private healthcare providers would do equally well tracking health statistics and indicators in order for effective strategic planning of infrastructure development and service offerings. Let us illustrate these points with one age-related health problem whose incidence is of increasing concern, falls among the elderly. About two-thirds of injury-related hospitalizations for seniors, result from injurious falls estimated to cost the country's health care system more than C$1 billion annually[13], and affected seniors and their families, disability, reduced quality of life and social contact, institutionalization, and reduced life span. Canada has a variety of data sources for seniors' falls. Key among these sources are epidemiological evidence on falls highlighting seniors' self-reported data from the Canadian Community Health Survey (CCHS), a component of the Population Health Survey Program of Statistics Canada, which gives estimates of health determinants, health status and health system utilization for the health regions nationwide. Other sources include; hospitalization data from the Canadian Institute for Health Information Discharge Abstract Database (DAD) for all seniors, then more specifically for seniors in residential care; and mortality data from Statistics Canada's Canadian Vital Statistics. There is evident convergence in the overall patterns of data from these various sources. Data from Cycle 2.1 of the CCHS, for example, shows that the survey sample of about 29,000 respondents for 2002/ 03 represents a population of about 3.8 million Canadians 65 years and above, with a median age of 72 years, and 56% of who were female[14]. The data also shows that relative to the entire population of seniors, those who have had an injurious fall were more likely to be; female (68% vs. 56%); aged, over 80 years (28% vs. 21%); widowed, separated or divorced (46% vs. 34%); to have post-secondary graduation (34% vs. 32%); and a household income of less than $15,000 (14% vs. 10%). The rate of injurious falls increased with age from 35 per 1000 population among seniors, 65-69 years old, to 76 per 1000 population in those 80 years and over. Female rates topped male rates in all age groups, and the differences for all rates are statistically significant but for the 75-79 age group. Respondents overall reported a fall-related injury in the past year, serious enough to limit normal activities, at a national average rate of 47.7 per 1000 population among persons 65 years and over. The treatment of many of these falls would in future likely be more, at least in part, in healthcare facilities outside the hospital. Treating seniors health problems, including falls in the comfort of their homes, and in the company of their loved ones, or in suitable facilities outside the traditional hospital setting, as much as possible, fosters a sense of independence, enhances quality of life, and saves healthcare costs. However, a major requirement for the success of such domiciliary or ambulatory care would be the implementation of appropriate healthcare ICT. Such technologies as would facilitate treatment, but also achieve other important treatment goals, including monitoring and evaluating care, alert systems to enable seniors receive urgent medical or nursing attention, and radio frequency identification (RFID) devices, which give seniors freedom to move around, but also enable caregivers to know where they are, ensuring they do not wander off are important. That the number of falls increased with age with the greatest increases among women is in keeping with previous studies[15, 16]. On the other hand, the increases

82

in the rate of falls by age and gender have social welfare, but also healthcare services implications. For example, the finding that the rates for women are statistically significantly higher than for men in every age group but one may reflect lower income, more social isolation and higher prevalence of chronic diseases among women, the latter, healthcare ICT could help in their prevention, prompt diagnosis and treatment, to relieve symptoms, and control or prevent their sequelae. These treatments say for arthritis or osteoporosis need not be in a traditional hospital setting, as indeed other conditions even simply age-related such as stroke, and dementia need not. Indeed, as with other chronic diseases, some of which for example diabetes also have associations with demographic factors, being more prevalent among immigrant populations, of African, and Hispanic descent, and among native Indians in the US and in Canada, ICT could help with their prevention, treatment, and rehabilitation, and reduce hospitalization rates, hence health spending on the diseases. Furthermore, what implications does the scarcity of relevant professional expertise, misdistribution of professionals, the average length of hospital stay for a fall injury being longer than for all causes of hospitalization for seniors 65 years and over by about 40%, and longer with age, have for the future management of falls in the elderly? In particular, with most falls although occurring at home, yet only 7.4% of individuals 65 years and older living in residential care settings[17, 18], in effect contributing the largest share to falls among seniors, what role could healthcare ICT play in preventing falls in these residential care settings? For example would seniors wearing a Memswear a jacket that uses MEMS (Micro-Electric Mechanical Systems) technology and is capable of calling for help when the wearer falls, and is being enhanced to even prevent the fall in the first place by warning the wearer via beeps or other means not help achieve this goal? Could this not save enormous hospital costs, even influence the planning, location, and structure of new health facilities? With the projected growth among the 85 and over age group in Canada being from 430,000 in 2001 to 1.6 million by 2041,[19] and people living longer with chronic conditions, what business opportunities do software and ICT firms envisage in developed countries, which would clearly be keen to reduce the increased hospitalization rates that these figures portend? Should software and ICT firms and others interested in the far-reaching implications of aging in Canada and other developed countries not also be interested in its geographic dimensions, exploring the demographic processes associated with aging on a provincial, territorial, or metropolitan scale, depending on the market theater, catchment areas of interest in order to conduct more meaningful strategic planning exercises? Would the interpretation of statistics on falls in the elderly or the prevalence and incidence of chronic diseases associated with aging not be more accurate and valuable considering the effects of age-in-place or net migration on aging for example? How do social and economic changes affect the direction and future of aging in a province, health region, even town and what bearings should the projections on aging in these circumstances have on health planning and service provision[20]? What might be the implications of these analyses for policy decisions on hospital construction or closure, on which ICT to implement and where, or on the need for certain specialized services and whether to develop or outsource them? Besides falls in the elderly, young people also represent a significant at-risk group for injuries of all sorts, particularly traumatic injuries, with significant implications for healthcare costs. However, it seems best to consider these injuries in the context of much wider health risk behaviors such as smoking, drinking, and using marijuana, related to peer-pressure, among other possible causes. There is no doubt that healthcare ICT could help with reducing the prevalence of these problems, some of which could result in physical and psychological health problems that could lead to increased health service utilization, including hospitalizations, and soaring health costs. As the foregoing shows, it is important to consider health indicators as determinants of future patterns of hospitalizations, and indeed, of the need for the development of more appropriate alternative health facilities. Is it appropriate to plan to build more hospitals when population-based health measures based on in-depth analyses of projected disease patterns and prevalence for example, are more-appropriate foci? On the other hand, closing hospitals down simply to contain health spending without such an exercise rooted in a deliberate evaluation and understanding of the relevant issues, and worse still not implementing the alternatives to that course of action would be just as inappropriate. The direction of health policy regardless, healthcare ICT would likely underpin the decision taken. To underscore that policy makers appreciate this point, the European Union recently awarded a $14 million grant to international researchers, led by the University of Newcastle, to develop further a biosensor to detect disease. This sensor uses similar technology to that used in navigation systems and care air bags, but with the vibrating disc just about the size of a dust speck. It recognizes cancer markers, distinctive proteins, or other molecules that cancer cells produce, and could aid the early diagnosis and effective monitoring of cancers and methicillin-resistant Staphylococcus aureus, or MRSA, for examples, which would no doubt reduce morbidities, even save many lives. Would the widespread use of such a biosensor not significantly influence the future of the hospital? For so long, the health industry has failed to seize the opportunities ICT offers that could improve the quality of health services delivery. It is now a new era. Healthcare seems poised for change, delivered by the increasingly sophisticated technologies, which seem to be inevitable final arbiters in even what it does with one of its most cherished institutions; the hospital.

References

1. Available at: http://www.camrosecanadian.com/story.php?id=204248
Accessed on: December 28, 2005

2. Ruckley CV. Socio-economic impacts of chronic venous insufficiency and leg ulcers. *Angiology* 1997; 48: 67-9.

3. Simon DA, Freak L, Kinsella A, Walsh J, Lanc C, Groarke L, et al. Community leg ulcer clinics: a comparative study in two health authorities. *BMJ* 1996; 312: 1648-51.

4. Available at:
http://www.canada.com/vancouversun/news/business/story.html?id=20b56a79-de7e-4d67-8e69-c65850923631&k=36198
Accessed on December 28, 2005

5. Available at: http://www.dailydemocrat.com/news/ci_3350638
Accessed on December 29, 2005

6. Available at: http://www.yolocounty.org/docs/MHSA-CSS-Plan.pdf
Accessed on December 29, 2005

7. Available at: www.cpa-apc.org
Accessed on December 29, 2005

8. Enthoven, AC., Tollen, LA., eds., Toward a 21st Century Health System: The Contributions and Promise of Prepaid Group Practice. San Francisco, Jossey-Bass, 2004

9. Available at: http://content.nejm.org/cgi/content/full/351/23/2458

10. P. Starr. *The Social Transformation of American Medicine* (New York: Basic Books, 1982.

11. E. H. Frech III, *Competition and Monopoly in Medical Care* (Washington, D.C.: AEI Press, 1996).

12. Mayo Clinic, "History"
Available at: http://www.mayoclinic.org/about/history.html

13. Available at: http://www.hc-sc.gc.ca/seniors-aines/index_pages/whatsnew_e.htm
Accesses on December 31, 2005

14. Available at: http://www.hc-sc.gc.ca/seniors-aines/pubs/seniors_falls/chapter2_e.htm
Accessed on December 24, 2005

15. Fletcher, P. C., and J. P. Hirdes. "Risk factors for falling among community-based seniors using home care services." Journal of gerontology, Vol. 57A, No. 8, 2002, pp. M504-M510.

16. Scott V.; S. Peck and P. Kendall. Prevention of falls and injuries among the elderly: A special report from the Office of the Provincial Health Officer. Victoria, B.C.: Ministry of Health Planning, 2004.

17. Health Canada. Canada's aging population. Ottawa: Division of aging and seniors, 2002.

18. Statistics Canada Census. 2001. Available at:
http://www12.statcan.ca/english/census01/Products/Analytic/companion/fam/canad a.cfm
Accessed on December 31, 2005

19. Peel, N. M.; D. J. Kassulke and R. J. McClure. "Population based study of hospitalized fall related injuries in older people." Injury prevention, Vol. 8, 2002, pp. 280-83.

20. Social and economic dimensions of an aging population (SEDAP)
Available at: http://socserv2.socsci.mcmaster.ca/~sedap/p/sedap97.pdf
Accessed on December 31, 2005

ICT and the Future of the Health Insurance Industry

Ford Motor Co announced on January 23, 2006 that it plans to lay-off 25,000 to 30,000 workers, and shut down 14 facilities by 2012. According to the company, the second largest automaker in the US, the plan is part of a restructuring effort to negate a $1.6 billion loss, it incurred in its North American operations in 2005. This is a significant development, not just for the auto but also the health, and insurance industries, and for the region's economy, if not that of the entire world. Just conceptualizing the effects this plan would have on the company's 122,000 employees in the region, between 20% and 25% of who would lose their jobs, including 1,200 in Canada, is numbing. Indeed, the United Auto Workers union President Ron Gettelfinger and Vice President Gerald Bantom, who directs the UAW National Ford Department, described it, in their reaction to the announcement, as "devastating.¹" The decision by Ford did not emerge spontaneously. In fact, there are ongoing negotiations between the company and the union, more scheduled for 2007, although the union and the company hold different views on the causes of the company's problems and their solutions. The company, as contained in its new "Way Forward" plan, wants to cut jobs and close facilities to align its production capacity with the dwindling demand for its vehicles. It also wants to cut material costs by $6 billion in five years, to streamline parts purchasing, and focus on the more fuel-efficient hybrid vehicles and smaller, sleeker, cars to respond to changing consumer tastes and concern over high gas prices. Ford wants to build on its 19% gain in fourth quarter earnings, which surpassed Wall Street expectations on performance at its finance arm and a lesser loss in the critical North American market, its shares gaining 6% upon the announcement. It plans to make its North American operations, which lost $143 million during the fourth quarter, profitable again by 2008, and projects that its market share would be stable by 2006. The union on the other hand claims that the company should have focused instead on expanding its market share in a highly competitive market via new and innovative product development. Besides, the reasons that the company and the UAW union advanced for Ford's decision, others adduce reasons such as increasing competition from Japanese automakers, and in particular, high pension and health care costs, the latter which also led General Motors Corp. to announce in November, 2005, its plans to slash 30,000 jobs and close down many of its plants. Indeed, some contend that Ford needs to provide investors more information on how it plans to turn its fortunes around. Specifically some are asking whether it could defend its market, the company's market share having slipped to 17.4%, excluding its luxury models, by the end of 2005, the lowest level since the late 1920s, or make early retirements match its pace of plant closures. These issues have profound implications for not only Ford, but also for the automotive industry as a whole, and in fact, beyond, for other industries as well, including the health and insurance industries. How for example, could Ford defend its market, particularly the mass market, where it is losing customers the most, shutting its plants down? Is the company planning to increase production capacity in fewer plants? Would it have enough plants for enough production volume to boost its market share in the highly competitive mass market, where Japanese automakers are already holding sway? Some would also argue that laying-off staff or forcing workers into early retirement is just as counter-intuitive as closing down its plants is counter-intuitive if the company planned to foray into a mass market with new products. Indeed, there would be others who would hold that what the company needs in order to reverse its fortunes is an experienced and dedicated workforce. Now, the question the company would pose is where the money comes from to pay the workers and take care of their various benefits, particularly their health benefits. There is no doubt that the question is pertinent. With regard health benefits, the insurance industry has a major role to play in helping companies contain health expenditures, hence making it unnecessary for them to resort to such drastic measures as those that Ford recently announced. How the insurance industry could do that, specifically via the use of information and communications technologies and the role that healthcare ICT plays in the industry regarding the delivery and economics of health services constitute the primary subject matter of this discussion. The question of why Ford Motor Co made its recent announcement is crucial, particularly those relating to healthcare insurance coverage for its workers, considering what lessons all involved could learn from it. Furthermore, could these lessons not help in teasing out what the future holds for its workers, particularly in relation to their healthcare coverage and those of their families and dependants? The UAW in the official statement referred to above, affirmed its intention to ensure the implementation to the letter of the coverage guaranteed in the job security program and all other provisions and protections of the UAW-Ford National Agreement. This would certainly augur well for the workers and their families. The question remains, however, with regard health, the extent, and duration of the health coverage of these workers, particularly post-retrenchment. Indeed, does this development not call for revisiting workers health insurance issues? Does it in fact not call for re-examining the dynamics between payers, and providers, not just regarding workers but the health insurance conundrum as a whole? What role does healthcare ICT play in all these? Could it have helped avert the Ford decision, for example? Are these roles different in public and private health insurance settings? How has ICT affected Canada's publicly funded health system, Medicare, or UK's National Health Service (NHS) for examples? How are these influences likely to change in the future? Is there a need for reappraisal of the place of ICT in the operations of the health insurance industry vis-à-vis healthcare providers and payers? How could this improve the bottom line for health insurance companies, while ensuring the provisions of comprehensive and qualitative care to workers and their dependants, and that the companies that sponsor their health insurance remain in business? What role does government play in all of these?

Consider the following. President Bush plans to limit health care costs by expanding tax-free Health Savings Accounts, which would allow individuals to set aside money for routine medical expenses. The plan, expected to feature in the President's Jan. 31, 2006, State of the Union address to Congress, complements his new prescription-drug benefit plan under the Medicare health program for elderly and disabled people, launched on Jan. 1, 2006. These two initiatives indicate not only an acknowledgement that there are problems with health insurance coverage in the US, but that they need fixing. There are of course those that do not agree with the President's initiatives for solving these problems, the above being only two, and implementing them could pose a new set of problems. For example, there are reports that administrative problems hamper the program's implementation, many eligible patients unable to have their prescription costs covered, problems many attribute to information systems flaws, which incidentally underline the important role of healthcare ICT in health insurance. Consider also the idea of pay-for-performance program, which actually has been around in the US for some time but is now gaining increasing favor. The initiative aims to reward doctors with bonuses for meeting certain standards of care. The bonuses, which range from $50 to $160 per patient per year, could add up to significant amounts in some practices. One of the hindrances to the adoption of ICT by physicians is the perception that health plans, insurers and patients, not the doctors benefit from these ICT investments. However, the pay-for-performance program seems to be a win-win situation as patients get higher quality care, doctors make money, and health plans that have often invested millions of dollars on healthcare ICT finally get doctors to adopt ICT and integrate it with the health plans systems. What s more, participating health plans save money through reduced hospital visits and unnecessary testing, bonuses regardless. The program has its critics though, who posit that some doctors might refuse to take on seriously ill patients because they do not want to compromise their scores. Nonetheless, the large firms, for examples Procter & Gamble and GE, determined to reduce healthcare costs, fully back the program. Indeed, an alliance of employers, payers, and providers launched the non-profit Bridges to Excellence in 2003, launching the program in Ohio, Kentucky, and Massachusetts, with measures in three areas, namely: diabetes care, cardiovascular care, and patient-care management systems. As more health plans embrace the program, its organizers are adding on new care standards in cancer care, asthma and pain management. A number of physician organizations, including the American Academy of Family Physicians and the Medical Group Management Association also support the program. In late march, 2005, the program got a new participant, CareFirst BlueCross BlueShield, which said that it would pay doctors up to $20,000 to install electronic patient records systems as part of its record-keeping bonus plan. The health plan s program would span 10 states and cover over 2 million individuals. What do President Bush s initiatives have in common with the pay-for-performance program? First, they both exemplify the efforts on the government s part on the one hand, and on the other, that of the private sector to tackle some of the core problems afflicting the US healthcare delivery system. They also illustrate the need for innovative ideas in addressing the complex interplay of factors involved in healthcare delivery in the country. They attest to the necessity for intersectoral collaboration in finding solutions to healthcare problems, and finally, highlight the important role healthcare ICT plays in health services and healthcare delivery. Speaking of intersectoral collaboration, there is also an important dimension, one that perhaps should interest all stakeholders the most. A recent long-term, population-based study published in the January issue of the American Journal of Psychiatry, has shown evidence that directly contradicts a 2004 U.S Food and Drug Administration (FDA) advisory that adults starting to use the newer antidepressants, have a higher risk of suicidal behavior2. The study, which aimed to evaluate the risk of suicide death and serious suicide attempt, employed computerized health plan records to identify 65,103 patients with 82,285 episodes of antidepressant treatment between Jan. 1, 1992, and June 30, 2003. The authors identified death by suicide using state and national death certificate data, and serious suicide attempt, that is, suicide attempt resulting in hospitalization, using hospital discharge data. The study not only showed that the risk of death by suicide was not significantly higher in the month following the commencement of the medication than in subsequent months, but also that the risk of suicide attempt was actually highest in the month prior to starting antidepressant treatment and declined progressively after treatment with the medication started. The study also revealed that the risk of suicide with the newer antidepressants reviewed by the FDA, ten in all, namely, bupropion, fluoxetine, citalopram, fluvoxamine, mirtazepine, nefazodone, paroxitine, sertraline, escitalopram, and venlafaxine, was lower than with the older antidepressants, and that suicide rates even declined faster with the newer medications. In other words, this study showed that taking the newer antidepressants means less likelihood of serious suicide attempts, and even more affirmatively, that taking the newer antidepressants do not increase one s risk of serious suicide attempts. What are the implications of this study for the insurance industry? Could it result in re-classification of actuarial risk factors and scores, updating premium pricing or changes in premium polices for certain individuals? Would these findings influence prescription patterns by doctors, possibly leading to a prescribing surge, even overuse of the medications, with cost implications for health plans and other payers? Does this study not highlight the important role of healthcare ICT in the insurance industry? Does it also not underscore the need for the industry to be conversant with research progress and other developments in the health industry, and the significance of the concept of intersectoral collaboration? What role does healthcare ICT play in the actualization of this concept? Is it more likely to play an increasing or decreasing role? A large, multicenter, prospective study conducted in five hospitals in Ontario, Canada, the results presented at the recent 47th annual meeting of the American Society of hematology in Atlanta, Georgia, showed that patients with lower leg fractures, that is, of the patella, fibula, tibia, ankle, or foot, very rarely develop venous thromboemboli (VTE), making the prophylactic prescription of anticoagulants unnecessary. The chances of developing deep venous thrombosis (DVT), a potentially life-threatening condition, in these patients previously reported being as high as 40%, doctors routinely prescribed anticoagulants for them. Again, what effect would this new finding have on such prescribing patterns? Would insurers revisit the terms of the policies of clients with diabetes for example, based on another recent finding published in the December 14, 2005 issue of the Journal of the American Medical Association, indicating an increased risk of pancreatic cancer in male smokers who have high insulin concentrations and resistance? Would such findings further hike the already rising private health insurance costs, costs that are increasing even in Canada, with an essentially, publicly funded health system? A Statistics Canada study released in mid-December 2005 showed that Canadians are paying more for private healthcare service. According to this study, they paid an average of C$1,690, roughly, 2.7% of their pay on private health services in 2004, a 6% increase over what they paid in 2003, the increase attributed to increases in eye care expenses, and in health insurance premiums. Residents of Alberta, who paid the most, in fact spent C$2,150 on out-of-pocket healthcare services, British Columbia residents, a close second, at C$2,080, and those of Prince Edward Islands in third place, at C$1,760 4. Are there steps, for example, health prevention measures that individual payers would likely be taking to reduce their out-of-pocket health insurance expenses? Could more intense screening programs for example, detect latent type II diabetes and prevent its ocular complications? How would such measures affect the insurance industry? Could the insurance industry be taking measures of its own to spread insurance risks round, easing the financial burden on payers while retaining the capacity of insurance firms to make profit? What role could healthcare ICT play in measures that individual payers, and insurance companies would take, and could there be a convergence of goals with neither party losing out consequent upon the deployment and harmonization of the appropriate ICT? The significance of these questions for all stakeholders in the health insurance industry could not have come out more forcefully than the former US Department of Health and Human

Services Secretary Tommy Thompson put it on Tuesday, January 26, 2006, at a health care conference in Washington, D.C. The former Secretary not only called for a nationwide shift to preventive care, but for employers to demand that their health care providers use ICT, examples of measures he advocated would help reduce healthcare costs, which for the US, currently $1.9 trillion, he projected would double in seven years without serious attention paid to the issues involved. Indeed, the former Secretary recommended specific measures to achieve this goal such as employers doubling the price of junk food in company cafeterias, having nutritionists on staff, requiring employees to exercise and charging smokers more for health insurances. Again, what role could healthcare ICT play in implementing some of these measures? The Secretary specifically singled out insurers and the federal government in not having done enough to educate the public. Could they indeed do more, and collaborate better in reducing this information asymmetry? How could such efforts enhance competition among healthcare providers, and how could this energize other market forces and reduce healthcare costs without necessarily compromising the quality of healthcare delivery? What role would healthcare ICT play in implementing, for example, the Secretary's recommendation of a common form that employees could use to enroll in health plans? It is clear from the discussion thus far how variegated, yet intercalated, health insurance issues are, as is the need for the insurance companies for ongoing evaluations of these issues, and in particular, the central roles that healthcare ICT would increasingly play regarding these issues vis-à-vis the insurance industry, in order to survive in an increasingly hyper-competitive business milieu. Let us explore the issues a little further.

Pricing is among the most important issues health insurance firms need to deal with in order to make profits and remain viable. Several factors determine pricing in the health insurance industry, but perhaps none should be more important than a thorough understanding of health issues. Diabetes, asthma, high blood pressure, and other diseases common in the developed world are major drivers of health care utilization costs, and could pose management challenges in order to reduce poor outcomes. Insurance firms need to understand current and evolving guidelines for the treatment of these conditions, and of disease conditions in general, and present and emerging therapeutic modalities for them, as the examples given above show. They also need to understand the approaches to preventing the sequelae of diseases, and how such measures influence actuarial risks, burden of disease on individuals, their families, and on society at large, and imminent and long-term measures to tackle these diseases both by individuals and health agencies, and what this means for their future prevalence, all important pricing issues. To buttress these points, a recent study published in the January 26, 2006 issue of the New England Journal of Medicine showed that black people and native Hawaiians are more likely than white people and others to develop lung cancer, even if they smoked the same number of cigarettes, up to a pack daily6. The study of over 180,000 people, over 50% of them minorities, showed that whites who smoked up to a pack daily had a 43% to 55% lower risk of lung cancer compared to blacks, Hispanics and Japanese-Americans, 60% to 80% less likely compared to blacks to develop lung cancer smoking up to a pack of cigarettes daily. Even Black, Hispanic and Japanese-American men who never smoked had higher risks of lung cancer than white men do with no significant differences between women in theses ethnic groups. The study also did not find differences in lung cancer risk among heavy smokers, who smoked over three packs a day, in the various ethnic groups. This study suggests that genes play a part and could help explain the racial differences in prevalence and mortality previously noticed in lung cancer. How would this new information affect health insurance policies and pricing? Would the insurance industry be interested to explore further the possible reasons for these racial differences before making those policies, and pricing changes? Some experts argue that the differences occur because of smoking habits, for example, that blacks tend to inhale more, receiving higher doses of carcinogens than whites do, and they have higher smoking rates, although whites smoke more per day. Would the insurance also avoid being embroiled in the controversy surrounding such studies and the effect of race on the risk of disease, in general, or use information emanating from them in policy formulation? Considering that genetics features increasingly in not just new drug developments, including in customizing medications to particular individuals, but also in screening and testing technologies, could insurance companies ignore these issues? Indeed, some already criticize this so-called geneticization of society on the score that insurance firms would use knowledge of DNA testing indicating that an individual has a diathesis toward a particular disease to discriminate against that person. Despite this and other criticisms, could insurance companies for example, ignore the fact that in 2005, the U.S Food and

Drug Administration (FDA) approved a heart-failure drug, BiDil, specifically for blacks7, or that in fact, researches have shown different response rates among certain ethnic groups to cancer drugs? Could insurance companies ignore research evidence that BiDil, a fixed-dose combination of isosorbide dinitrate and hydralazine hydrochloride, could help reduce morbidities among the roughly 750,000 African Americans that have heart failure, an incurable condition over half of those that have which die within five years of diagnosis? What effect is the "new genetics" going to have on the insurance industry in both the short-and long-terms, including, regarding issues such as cloning? Have insurance firms started considering what effects, other emerging technologies such as in stem cell research would have on the industry? There is no doubt from the foregoing that health insurance firms need to keep abreast of progress in medical research in order to have competitive pricing polices. It must be clear that this is not going to be an easy task, but the appropriate use of ICT, for example, the use of data mining technologies, and expert input, from within or outside the firm to analyze data and information and convert them into actionable knowledge could help in realizing this crucial objective. Significantly also, for this task to be meaningful, it has to be ongoing, as medical progress is what it is, progress, and these days, is some would say, at a frenetic pace, considering the increasing exploitation of information technologies in medical research at all levels, clinical and academic, inclusive. In view of the ever-competitive nature of the healthcare industry, insurance firms could pool resources in order to minimize the sometimes-substantial costs involved in implementing the relevant technologies, and in the end, the return on investment (ROI) of such moves should not be difficult to compute. Do these issues also not highlight the need for intersectoral collaboration mentioned earlier, considering the eclectic sources these data and information would come from? How could such collaboration be possible without information sharing, and how could information be cost-effective without cutting-edge ICT? There is therefore no doubt that an integral part of the survival of health insurance firms in contemporary times is to have a comprehensive ICT strategy that is in consonance with its overall vision and tailored to meet specific new process and process-improvement goals. The Wall Street Journal on January 25, 2006, examined the issue of collaboration among stakeholders to gather, share, and use valuable health information in the interest of all. In what the paper described as a "growing national effort", to rake through electronic health records to gain data for research, safety assurance, and best-practice identification, it profiled two intensive-care databases used for pediatricss. One, maintained by Paediatrix Medical in Florida, utilizes a system that monitors newborns' vital signs to feed statistics into an enormous electronic documentation system. The National Institutes of Health (NIH) and the FDA, for examples have requested the use of the information to test the efficacy of antibiotics, which is useful as evidence of best practices. Vermont-Oxford Network, a Burlington, Vt.-based not-for profit, has a similar system used to determine whether quality improvement training and performance feedback increase the utilization of lifesaving therapy in intensive care units (ICUs.) The company plans to send out alerts for best-practice guidelines to hospitals and physicians using this system anytime soon. Should insurance companies not be looking into collaborating with such organizations or building databases of their own, which they could update in real-time, in order to have current and competitive pricing and premium policies? How do they plan to counter the perception in certain quarters that such databases and data mining only help insurers and employers obtain personal information about people's medical history that they could use against them down the road? Would insurers consider for example embracing emerging technologies that could strip all identifying data from the records to address such concerns? The US Agency for healthcare and Research Quality (AHRQ) for example, is currently sponsoring the use of "de-identified" data to study the benefits and risks of medications for diseases such as arthritis and cancer. Is it imperative for all stakeholders to come to terms with the increasing digitalization of patient records, and the likely rising use of such data and information by various government agencies, even private companies, including insurance firms, for crucial decision making? Is it equally mandatory for those that have access to such information, including health insurance firms, to reassure whose information they access about the privacy and confidentiality of the information via the use of such "de-identification" technologies? Does this again, not emphasize the need for insurance firms to have appropriate ICT strategies? The issue of post-mastectomy breast reconstruction led to the enactment of the Women's Health and Cancer Rights Act of 1999. Some believe that this resulted from the reluctance by insurance firms to cover a procedure they largely regard as cosmetic. This issue is yet another example of the need for an intersectoral approach by insurance companies, in developing their pricing and other policies. With the Act's added regulations for erring insurers in 2001, would insurance companies not be interested in changes in utilization patterns, for example relative to the 20% of eligible clients that had this procedure despite its benefits on quality of life prior to 2001? Insurance companies would probably also be interested in the factors that influence usage patterns, for example demographics, provider bias, patient preference, and barriers to care[9,10], factors that could help resolve a number of coverage issues, and on which collaboration with providers to share information, which healthcare ICT would facilitate, is undoubtedly important. Still on pricing and the factors that determine them, health insurers cannot ignore how providers price their products and services. This is even more so in an increasingly customer-directed business milieu. It would be unlikely surprising to find these clients, particularly those of them that are self-paying asking questions regarding variations in list prices across hospitals, sometimes even within the same neighborhoods. Should insurers not also query variations in bills from providers? Do some hospitals charge different payers different prices for similar goods and services? Should insurance companies not be interested in why such practices that could undermine their profitability exist? How could technology-backed compliance with regulated accounting practices help curb such practices? With some hospitals' chargemasters, the list of their prices for every procedure performed and for every supply item it consumed, sometimes having as many as 30, 000 items, there would be need for insurers and hospitals to collaborate on information sharing. By standardizing the format of chargemasters this is a process that the Health Insurance Portability and Accountability Act (HIPAA) of 1996 should facilitate and, indeed possibly eliminate the allegations by some that insurers actually pay far less to providers than the bills they receive from them. What seems to stand out distinctly then is the need not just for insurers but also for providers to have sophisticated healthcare ICT that would streamline the billing process, avoid sporadic, and inconsistent updates of an annual process, making it more efficient and effective, and chargemasters made public, but easier to understand, for clients, thus creating a win-win situation. This may require insurers collaborating among themselves to minimize the multiplicity of third-party contract terms between them and providers. Here again, healthcare ICT providing not just information sharing and communication technologies but also those that furnish insurers with up-to-date information on progress in medicine would facilitate the standardization of approaches to pricing, billing and premiums terms, and compensation issues, among other health insurance operations.

Whether it is national health insurance as in Canada and the UK, universal health insurance as in Germany, or any other health insurance financing model, there would always be the need to control and contain health costs. This is another major issue, which the health insurance industry would need to confront head-on in the years ahead. This is because the industry stands little chance of surviving unless it supports its partners in their efforts to survive. In other words, the health industry could not survive at the rate at which healthcare costs are escalating. How then could the health insurance industry survive? True, some health plans in the US, driven by member retention and service improvement are offering new banking services to their consumer-directed health plan members in 2006. Blue Cross Blue Shield Association's branded debit card with Visa and a comparable deal between American Express and WellChoice, parent company of Empire Blue Cross Blue Shield are some of the latest such banking-oriented services that health plans have launched. Another is BCBSA's formation of a Blue Healthcare Bank to provide BCBS firms and clients of their CDHPs or health savings accounts, flexible spending accounts or health reimbursement programs, with administration and financial backing, an initiative that has so far attracted thirty-one of thirty-nine plans. Are these moves "back-ups" of sorts, in the event of a crisis in the healthcare industry, even with members being enrollees of the plans? It is clear that there would be no enrollees, except of course those self-paying ones, were the companies providing health coverage for them to run aground. This introduces an added dimension to the issue of the survival of the health insurance industry, that of the survival of the employers paying the premiums for their workers. Could the insurance industry imagine Ford Motor Co. or General Motors folding up? What if Wal-Mart collapsed and government declared as it recently did regarding the automotive industry, that there would be no 1970s, Chrysler-style bailouts? These banking initiatives are exercises in collaboration that the insurance industry needs to extend to other critical areas of their interactions, this time with partners outside the insurance and finance sectors. They also exemplify what ICT could achieve in terms of the value propositions to their customers, for examples, easy and hassle-free payment options, deductions tracking, and greater power over their healthcare spending decisions. Nonetheless, the symbiotic relationships between the health insurance industry and payers and providers, including suppliers, means that each constituent of this complex and dynamic association needs to ensure that the others survive to ensure its own continuity. Indeed, this association reflects the organic nature of society as a whole, a fully functional entity, each of whose components breathes life into it, and without which on the aggregate, it slowly withers away. In addition to traditional economic approaches, for examples, cost sharing and shifting, managed care and competition, and remuneration controls, although some contend that managed care incentives merely shift costs and do not help control overall health costs, there is an ongoing need for new ideas from all stakeholders, including from the insurance industry on ways to control health costs. In particular, there needs to be more emphasis on improving the quality of healthcare delivery, via the more-widespread use of clinical practice guidelines, encouraging competition among healthcare providers with new ICT, and the ongoing evaluation of such technologies, and their effects on health outcomes. Other medical strategies such as health services regionalization, sound recruitment and retention policies, and exploration of options in healthcare delivery, including those that would help with resource optimization, among others should feature prominently on the agenda of policy makers in the health insurance industry, as moves that the industry would have to re-organize itself to endorse and help to actualize. There is no gainsaying the need for insurance firms to remain solvent, which may sometimes be at odds with the desire of their clients to stay healthy but the two are not in the least incompatible. In other words, supporting government or companies in their bids to control health costs in fact, is in keeping with the long-term survivability of the insurance industry. This is not to say that the industry should support efforts to undermine health services delivery, which would be antithetical to their goals, a scenario not difficult to see. Suppose for example that due to government's lack of interest or overly cost-curtailing measures, it did not implement the necessary prevention and response measures against for example, an imminent epidemic, with the result that it affected let us even say, a third of the country's workforce. Would insurance firms not bear perhaps the most significant portion of the economic burden of this epidemic, even with re-insurance cover? It is therefore clear the delicate position that the insurance industry occupies in the scheme of things. Governments no doubt have a role to play in providing the enabling environment for the private sector, including the insurance industry, to participate in the efforts to reduce health costs, while ensuring qualitative healthcare delivery to all, and many are. Indeed, since the days of the 1993 *Government Performance and Results Act"*, the 1996 *Information Technology Management Reform Act"* and, the *National Performance Review"* (now the *National Partnership for Reinvention*) under the Clinton administration, the U.S has demonstrated a more serious commitment to collaborating with the private sector in achieving its goals of reducing costs, improving efficiency and ensuring accountability. With efforts initially concentrated on procurement reform, new and more flexible purchasing and negotiating models emerged that promoted increased private-sector participation in the decision-making process and pay for performance predicated on result-based contracts. The 1980s and 1990s witnessed the outsourcing of non-core functions to the private sector, from basic support functions such as printing, to the ICT operations of an entire city. Thus the insurance industry could collaborate with the public sector in reducing healthcare costs investing in sophisticated ICT infrastructure and technical expertise in rectifying information asymmetry, and facilitating the adoption of electronic health records (EHR) by healthcare providers, even if it had to impose a fee on premium services, and relinquish control over data sources to government. The industry would be making more of its clients healthy, a sizeable number of people in the US for example with a workforce of 147 million people, thus increasing its chances of profitability. It would also be acquiring even more technical expertise by being primed to exploit technological progress in meeting competition, and would be helping reduce overall government budget on health. More broadly, it would also directly, or otherwise be helping government's goals of making local firms competitive even against foreign insurers that could come into the country to do business, and in an increasingly global market, in which the industry has a serious stake anyway. More recently in the U.S, the House Ways and Means Health Subcommittee Chair Nancy Johnson (R-Conn.) and Commerce Health Subcommittee Chair Nathan Deal (R-Ga.) on October 27, 2005, introduced a bill (HR 4157) that would allow the Department of Health and Human Services (HHS) to develop national medical privacy standards, and ease limitations on donating ICT equipment to doctors. It would also require HHS to adopt data transaction standards, and billing codes, and to examine the effect of state privacy laws and data transaction standards on the flow of medical data, and report within 18 months on "whether state and federal privacy laws should be conformed to a single set of federal standards," a summary of the bill states. If HHS affirmed the need for such standards, Congress would enact, within three years, the standards or the HHS would have the authority to create a uniform system for health information privacy and security. By allowing, "Hospitals, group practices and other entities to provide physicians with hardware, software, or [IT] training and support services that are used primarily for the electronic exchanges of clinical health information", this bill essentially opens the door to the private sector, including the insurance industry, to participate in promoting wider ICT diffusion in the health industry. Indeed, by also disallowing hospitals and other donors from trying to control how doctors use the technology or prevent them from linking to other IT systems, and demanding that donated IT applications comply with HHS technology standards or certification procedures, the bill further creates the necessary milieu for information sharing, and the interoperability this requires. Overall, it appears that the bill would facilitate the achievement of the more widespread use of healthcare ICT, and the HHS has three years to study the effect of the provisions for "safe harbors" in the bill on the adoption of IT and "any impact it has had on business relationships between providers." Furthermore, the bill would codify the Office of the National Coordinator for Health Information Technology at HHS, and require it to maintain and update "a strategic plan to guide the nationwide implementation of interoperable health [IT] to improve health care quality, reduce medical errors, increase efficiency of care, and advance the delivery of appropriate evidence-based health care services". As further proof of government s commitment to involve the private sector in its healthcare ICT diffusion efforts, on September 13, 2005, Health and Human Services (HHS) Secretary Mike Leavitt announced the membership for the American Health Information Community, formed to help advance efforts to attain President Bush s objective for most Americans to have electronic health records (EHR) within a decade. The Community is a federally chartered commission. It will provide input and advise HHS on ways to facilitate the digitalization, and interoperability of health records, and assure their privacy and security, in a smooth, market-led way. The 17-member community has key leaders in the public and private sectors, including Scott Serota, President/ CEO of Blue Cross

Blue Shield Association. Examples of such government's efforts to encourage public-private sector collaboration abound in other countries too. Canada s alternate service delivery (ASD) received its official government endorsement in 1997, and government has progressively moved further into the public-private partnership (PPP) realm ever since in its approach to service delivery, including in the health sector. Besides increasing public outcry over rising healthcare costs, and hospital wait times, market liberalization, e-commerce, and technological progress are increasingly becoming inevitable change drivers in the country, which is exploring different public service delivery models, and with regard healthcare, particularly in the provinces and territories, Alberta s "Third Way" model, one example. NavCan and CFIA, in air control, and food inspection management respectively were early government-initiated, collaborative efforts, and many have followed in the construction, infrastructure design, and transportation sectors, among others. Of note in the healthcare ICT sector is a major project in Quebec, in which the *Commission de santé et sécurité au travail* (CSST) coupled with a private consortium to build an extranet that connects major companies, hospitals, rehabilitation centers, and CSST work accident victims in order to accelerate claims processing. Another is the Toronto Children's Hospital Internet portal that provides information to young patients, and their families, and shares patient information with other agencies, hospitals, and clinics. Indeed, all health regions in Canada now have Internet patient information portals. While some would construe the increasing involvement of the private sector, including the insurance industry, in public health projects as leading to privatizing the country s cherished Medicare, others would likely see it not just as the imperative antidote to rising healthcare costs, but also an expected consequence of the recent Supreme Court s decision to permit private healthcare in Quebec. Yet others, also as an inevitable consequence of the changing global economic climate in which the country must compete. The eventual direction that the country would go and the extent to which it would pursue its PPP objectives remain conjectural. In Australia, the government adopted the *Develop Australia Bonds* program and issued tax- shielding bonds to support the infrastructure projects that the private sector undertook, which between 1992 and 1996, accounted for a total of A$29 billion, a clear evidence of the private sector s interest in such a collaboration strategy. T he Australian government substantially funds both its public and private health systems via taxes, and the Medicare levy, charged at between 1.5% and 2.5% of taxable income. Although State and Territory Governments deliver and manage public health services and regulate health care providers, the Federal government collaborates with them to fund public hospitals, which provide most emergency and critical care facilities. The Federal government also collaborates with research agencies in public and private sectors, its commitments to which the allocation of A$41 billion to the sector in 2004 attests, over twice as much as in 1999, and a reflection of the increasing health spending, for example, from 15% to over 20% of the Federal Budget since 1996. The Australian Government also recently committed A$42 million to fund cutting-edge research and to foster collaboration between researchers, both in public and private sectors, A$9.25 million of which will fund five new health-related research networks that will investigate areas that the Government recognizes as National Research Priorities, which include the development of new biotechnology tools and health diagnostics. The country has a thriving private health care sector, which provides both health services and health insurance, and operates both for-and not-for-profit. Private health insurance is a significant part of the sector and covers part or all of hospital charges, medical fees and other health-related services. It is therefore not hard to see the reason for the increasing collaboration between these sectors. The UK has a long history of involving the private sector in public service delivery. The Thatcher government implemented an enormous privatization program in the early 1980s. It launched its successful *Private Finance Initiative* (PFI) in 1993 to facilitate public-private alliances for infrastructure projects, that made it possible to contribute via preferential loans, equity capital, asset transfers, and subsidiary work, singly or in combinations, agreements made between 1995 and 1996 valued at £ 5 million pounds. Transformed into Public-private partnerships (PPPs), resulting in the creation of the *Treasury Task Force,* the FPI program became more flexible, more accessible, and incurred much less transaction costs. The British government continues to embrace the PPP track, in particular two promising formulas, *joint ventures,* and *wider markets.* With the former, both public and private sectors invest in the project and share accrued profits or losses, and with the latter, an emphasis on marketing certain government-owned products using private-sector expertise in a specific area, one especially suited for and applied to ICT projects. Protagonists of these policies remain convinced that such collaborations cut costs, improve the quality of services, and free the public sector to concentrate on its core mission, and benefit the private sector in many ways, including risk mitigation, human resource development, and increased market opportunities, among others. There are of course many, who would argue against the outcomes of such public-private collaborations in the health sector, particularly regarding the controversy the country s mix of public and private healthcare continues to generate.

The onus seems to be on the insurance industry to do whatever it could to support health costs control, while simultaneously ensuring that these control do not compromise the health of their clients. This would help minimize concerns in certain circles over the real motives of collaboration between the industry with government agencies and in public health projects. The efforts of the insurance industry should therefore resoundingly be toward ensuring cost-effective yet qualitative healthcare delivery. The industry could achieve this dual objective relying on healthcare ICT. A quick example is the role that the Internet is playing in helping rectify the information asymmetry that pervaded both the health and health insurance industries prior to lately. It is counterintuitive to assume that that situation would not eventually compromise the average value of the products and services that these industries provide, regardless of their quality, and perhaps result in the markets for them dwindling, with possibly serious adverse consequences. For example, people might resort to the use of untested, even dangerous remedies, rather than as they see it, getting ripped off. Would it not in fact be better for all, including the insurance industry that fewer people become ill? Should the health industry, which seems to be benefiting from this healthcare ICT serendipity, not proactively explore further ways by which it could benefit even more from it? In a public-funded health insurance setting, the question of ex-post moral hazard is real, as individuals could overuse services that either they do not have to pay for or that government heavily subsidizes, although there would not be much to worry about regarding adverse selection. However, with as a significant population self-sponsored health insurance, what could the insurance industry do to resist the lure of increasing premiums that ex-post moral hazard could engender in response to government s efforts to reduce out-of-pocket expenditures on health insurance? Premiums are generally lower for health insurance applicants who do not smoke and live a demonstrably healthy life style. Indeed, insurance firms even offer such persons discounts. Is one way insurance firms could help reduce healthcare costs therefore not actively promoting such healthy lifestyles? How could the use of healthcare ICT help insurance firms achieve this goal? How might the bottom line of an insurance firm look down the road that actively promotes healthy living, perhaps even has "Wellness clinics" that qualifies clients that attend for some sort of incentive, for example discounts on their premiums? Could such a program attract more clients, and give the firm a competitive edge? Is a health insurance firm more viable the higher its number of healthy clients? How could such programs, if they became more widespread help in increasing the number of individuals with insurance coverage, making the populace healthier, and increasing productivity, and economic prosperity? Does not everyone gain in the end from a program such as this that may initially seem to lack face validity? The foregoing should not imply that only private insurance firms have the responsibility to help reduce healthcare costs. In fact, public health insurance perhaps has even more responsibility in this regard. Without a doubt, the case of the Veterans Health Administration (VHA) clearly shows that government health agencies might even outperform those in the private sector in terms of the delivery of cost-effective and qualitative health services. The universal, integrated system of VHA covers all aspects of healthcare, no veteran exempt, and VHA has deployed sophisticated billing and supply management and electronic health records (EHR) systems that streamline its processes, minimize labor wastage, reduce medical errors, and medication costs, hence reduce costs without compromising quality. Some contend that the VHA model is the way forward for healthcare delivery, and not private health systems[11]. Is this position garnering support in the US, where a recent survey of 1,104 adults, which the Center for American Progress in collaboration with Americans for Healthcare conducted, showed that 89% support the need for "fundamental changes" to address rising health costs and declining quality of care, 86%, support for reforms that would provide affordable health care for all? Support for "universal health care" among the same respondents dropped to 49%, and 37% actually withdrew support, when informed separately about arguments that such reforms translate to more government involvement or higher taxes[12]. However, on considering arguments from both sides of the universal health care debate, 84% supported reforms that would lead to universal health care, and 52%, said that they would support them, higher taxes and a larger government role, regardless. This survey shows that Americans want their health system reformed, and available to all, but divided on overly government involvement and higher taxes. The question then is how to achieve universal health coverage, with minimal regulation, and tax hikes, although some would argue that Sweden and Finland are welfare states yet provide quality health and social services, and have low unemployment rates. Could others not argue, though that the high taxes of these countries are a downside, especially as they are actually beginning to inconvenient individuals and cripple businesses in an increasingly global economy? Such efforts by the insurance industry as those mentioned earlier are no doubt important, which also highlights the need for the sort of intersectoral collaboration also earlier mentioned, wherein, other stakeholders for example also initiate healthy living programs, the cumulative effect of which would be a healthier society, with more universal health insurance coverage. What is more, this coverage would be qualitative, and cost-effective, reducing overall healthcare costs, obviating the need for higher taxes, and overarching government regulations. In other words, it is still possible to reduce health costs simultaneously delivering qualitative healthcare to all with the active involvement and collaboration of all stakeholders including the insurer, whether public or private. Indeed, such involvement by the insurance industry would help debunk the claim by some that health insurance and healthcare delivery are in fundamental and perpetual conflict. It is difficult to see how this easy it is to achieve this desirable state of affairs cost-effectively without the use of appropriate healthcare ICT. The success of the VHA shows that an organization could save substantially in administrative costs implementing such ICT, not to mention the enormous benefits that could accrue from implementing clinical information systems such as electronic health records (EHR), or computerized physician order entry (CPOE), or sophisticated health surveillance systems that could help prevent catastrophic epidemics, even pandemics. The involvement of the insurance industry in the future of the health industry is unlikely negotiable, if the both industries would survive. The complexity of healthcare service provision guarantees rising costs except all concerned act appropriately to curtail these costs. The insurance industry being a key play in healthcare service provision has a major role in averting a doomsday scenario. Besides encouraging the implementation of healthcare ICT among its ranks, to improve its operations and establish relevant communication and information sharing links, by developing innovative programs and even technologies in collaboration with software and ICT companies for example, it could help create the right milieu for achieving the goals of healthcare costs control. It could also help ensure that these costs reductions do not compromise the quality of healthcare delivery. Furthermore, by helping to increase the numbers of individuals with health insurance coverage, at affordable costs, it reduces their out-of-pocket expenses on healthcare, and makes more of their funds available for savings, and investment, both essential determinants of the rate and pattern of economic growth. In other words, the health insurance industry would also be contributing to the country s chances of accelerated economic growth, poverty obliteration, and indeed, sustainable economic development. The ongoing World Economic Forum (WEF) in Davos, Switzerland, 25-29 January, 2006, with over 2,000 of the world s most prominent political, business, labor union and religious leaders, among others in attendance, is testimony to the realization of the need for intersectoral collaboration in solving the problems of our age, as the original charter establishing the WEF states. Its emphasis on the creative imperative stresses the need for out-the-box thinking in order to tackle successfully, many of the challenges confronting contemporary society, particularly in the area of healthcare financing. The health insurance industry needs to continue to develop innovative approaches to make their involvement in healthcare delivery, be it in a publicly funded, privately funded, or mixed, health system, meaningful. About 50 million Americans for example, one-third of the workforce, change jobs, annually, many involving changes in locations. The situation is not much different in other developed countries. What is the implication of this mobile workforce for the health and insurance companies and for sustainable economic development? Indeed, could there be economic growth without jobs being available? Put differently, would there be jobs if companies ran aground due to government overregulation, excessive taxes, or lack of cooperation by the health insurance industry in supporting healthcare costs-curtailing measures, for examples? Is not the private sector that should be in the business of creating jobs, and the government of providing the enabling environment for this purpose? In other words, is job creation a core function of government? How would the demise of the employer affect the future viability of the insurance industry? Is there a compelling reason for the insurance company to be interested in the survival of the companies that pay their bills, or for that matter, government? There is no doubt that the insurance industry has an important stake in healthcare delivery beyond making profits. Indeed, the resolution of a whole set of healthcare delivery issues hinges on the involvement and performance of the insurance industry, and many of these issues are increasingly outside its customary domain. Take the question of the mobility of labor for example. T he worker that leaves Toronto for a new job in Vancouver for example would probably also have to change healthcare providers, and insurers, public and/or private. Would it not be easier and cheaper for this transition to occur were a seamless transfer of the worker s health records from one place to another possible? Could healthcare ICT not facilitate such transfers efficiently and cost-effectively? How could this occur without all involved, insurer, providers, pharmacists, opticians, podiatrist, for examples, able to communicate at all, and better still, electronically? Does this not suggest the need for not only insurance firms being "wired" but also healthcare providers, and the others involved in the individual s health service provision? Would the implementation of such healthcare ICT as would enable seamless data and information sharing among these various services not make service provision cheaper and more efficient ultimately? This case scenario also underlines the need for intersectoral collaboration. What could government do acting alone, for example, about the increasing mobility of labor, both within and between jobs and localities, and of capital concerning human resources provision, and changing healthcare needs, hence costs? Would collaborating with the private sector, including the insurance industry, in promoting the more widespread diffusion of healthcare ICT not help with not only understanding the important underlying dynamics of this movement of labor, including immigration, but also in reducing associated healthcare costs while at the same time ensuring the provision of qualitative health services? What are the implications of educational disparities, demographic changes, and opportunities or lack thereof for small and medium-sized enterprises (SMEs,) availability or otherwise of jobs, and pensions and taxation, for the health and insurance industries? What do the increasing trend toward Knowledge and Engineering Process Outsourcing (EPOs and KPOs) mean for internal job markets? Do they mean that insurers should prepare for job cuts, hence loss of clientele? Would companies have to continue being responsible for the health benefits of persons no longer in their payroll? What do all these mean for health insurers? These and other issues, many of which are not traditionally core insurance issues are now fundamental to the future of the industry. Experts are predicting an increasing demand for individuals with vocational training for example. What does this portend for labor mobility, and for the need for healthcare ICT ? The momentum for change in the health and health insurance industries is now in top gear. The Technology CEO Council in the US, a coalition of technology company officials founded in 1989, including Hewlett-Packard, Unisys, NCR, IBM, Dell, Motorola and Applied Materials, on October 12, 2005, released a report indicating that healthcare quality ¨suffers¨ and costs have increased due to the healthcare industry not implementing electronic health records (EHR) systems. The group strongly advocates implementing an EHR system to streamline the exchange of medical information among physicians, patients, laboratories, hospitals, and health insurers, noting that this would reduce health care costs by reducing duplication of lab tests, and administrative costs. The group, highlighting the need for collaborative effort, also noted that EHR would facilitate best practices and increase the quality of healthcare delivery, with information shared on the most effective treatments, medications and surgeries, and called on the federal government to help develop standards for health care ICT products. It also advised companies to decide on hiring or firing health insurers and providers partly on their use of healthcare ICT, and their ability to measure the quality of the services that they provide, and states to offer doctors and other healthcare providers, pecuniary incentives to use healthcare ICT. Governments are investing more in healthcare ICT. In October 2005, HHS officials announced the award of three contracts worth US$17.5 million to three private organizations to expand the use of EHR and develop standards for EHR product regulation. HHS awarded a US$3.3 million contract to the American National Standards Institute to develop software standards to enable providers to share health care information, and a US$2.7 million contract to the Certification Commission for Health Information Technology to develop standards for EHR products certification. It also awarded a US$11.5 million contract to the Health Information Security and Privacy Collaboration to establish health care privacy regulations. According to David Brailer, U.S National Coordinator for Health Information Technology, the contracts constitute a major step forward in achieving the goal of encouraging technical innovation for nationwide exchange of accurate, timely, and secure health information and EHR adoption. At about the same time, HHS Agency for Healthcare Research and Quality (AHRQ) awarded over US$22.3 million to 16 providers to implement health care IT systems. The selected grant recipients included eleven organizations from small and rural communities, from a group of agency grantees who received health care IT planning funds in 2004, part of AHRQ's goal being to learn from health IT implementation in clinical settings, as a means to facilitate greater healthcare ICT diffusion. Implementation cost is a key barrier to ICT adoption in the health industry, particularly in physician practices, and in small and rural hospitals, according to a recent survey released in October 2005, by the American Hospital Association. The healthcare insurance industry has many opportunities to help, and many firms in the industry have already started, to promote healthcare ICT adoption by also offering providers financial incentives. Health insurers also need to continue to develop innovative health promotion programs such as Silver Sneakers, which some health insurers sponsored for seniors, a creative blend of physical activity, healthy lifestyle and socially oriented programming that enables older adults to take greater control of their health. There are other programs such as water aerobics, and other less strenuous wellness and fitness programs increasingly common in the developed world designed for seniors. Such programs are in conformity with the idea of keeping clients as healthy as possible in order to reduce morbidity, hence reduce healthcare costs. It is would be counter-intuitive for insurers not to involve seniors in such programs by insurers and indeed, not to involve healthcare ICT in any cost-reducing effort, and it matters little whether the insurance is private or publicly funded, considering that seniors consume a significant portion of the rising health costs in many developed countries. Take Canada, for example. The projection for Canada's health care spending is C$142.0 billion in 2005, a 7.7% increase over 2004, a real inflation-adjusted rise of 5.0%, according to Canadian Institute for Health Information (CIHI) annual report on health care spending in Canada, *National Health Expenditure Trends 1975–2005* released on December 07, 2005[13]. The new estimates also reveal that health care spending continues, as a percentage of the country's gross domestic product (GDP) is also increasing, 7.0% in 1975, 10.0% by 1992, with a slight fall to 8.9% in 1996, and then rose again to 10.2% in 2004, CIHI projecting a further rise to an estimated 10.4% in 2005, its highest ever. With healthcare spending in fact growing faster than its economy, would the country not be seeking ways to reduce healthcare costs? The reports also showed that private sector health spending in 2005 is growing faster than public sector spending, and projections estimate this trend to increase by 8.7% over 2004, compared to an estimated 7.3% increase in public sector spending. However, public and private shares of total health care spending remained almost the same over the last five years, the former about 69.6% of total health care spending in 2005, compared to 70.0% in 2001 and 69.6% in 2002. Public sector spending billed to reach $98.8 billion in 2005, increased from $74.7 billion in 2001, most of the funds spent on hospitals and physicians. Estimates of private sector health care spending, essentially insurance and out-of-pocket expenditures, are $43.2 billion for 2005, an increase from $32.0 billion in 2001, with over half going toward drugs and dentistry, spending on public health, expected to be about $7.8 billion in 2005, compared to $406.8 million in 1975, $1.5 billion in 1985 and $3.3 billion in 1995. Some would ascribe the increasing private sector spending to the fallout from the increasing difficulties of provincial and territorial governments to cope with the increasing healthcare costs, hence reducing coverage under Medicare, de-insured services spilling over into private health insurance. However, with increasing spending on public health, which includes spending on prevention and health promotion, many programs enabled by healthcare ICT, and the active collaboration of health insurers in such programs, as with the seniors initiatives mentioned earlier, healthcare costs would likely fall via reduction in morbidities from chronic diseases and reduced hospitalization rates for examples. Indeed, insurers would still make profits, considering the likely reduction of their revenues that they would pay out. Per capita spending in 2005 was $4,411, a rise of 6.9% in over 2004, 4.2%, adjusted for inflation, slightly up from the 4.0% increase estimated for 2004, but less than that of 5.6% in 2001. Alberta ($4,820), spent the most on healthcare per person, followed by Manitoba ($4,790) and Ontario ($4,595), the least spenders being Quebec ($3,878), Prince Edward Island ($4,132) and British Columbia ($4,317). Because it is more expensive to provide health services for geographically dispersed populations, Yukon Territory, the Northwest Territories, and Nunavut spent much more. Should insurers not be interested to know the reasons for these differences in per capita spending? Could more widespread use of telemedicine and other appropriate healthcare ICT help reduce healthcare costs in the territories? Compared to other Organization for Economic Co-operation and Development (OECD) countries in US dollars, United States spent the most per capita ($5,635) in 2003, the latest year for which data are available, followed by Norway, Switzerland, and Canada, with per capita spending of $3,807, $3,781, and $3,001, respectively. Turkey spent the least per capita on health care ($513), just below Mexico ($583). It is obvious from the figures that Canada is one of the highest spenders on healthcare among OECD countries, and as the other figures showed, is spending increasingly more on the healthcare of its peoples. Most of the funds go into hospitals, about 30% of total health expenditure, estimated spending for 2005, $42.4 billion, up 6.4% from 2004, compared to $32.5 billion in 2001. Expenditures on drugs also significant, and the fastest-growing category of health spending, almost 18% of the healthcare budget, increased 11.0% from 2004, and is actually increasing faster than overall health expenditure, expected to increase to $24.8 billion in 2005, compared to $16.7 billion in 2001, most, 83%, prescribed drugs. Here again, the health insurance industry could help to reduce these costs by encouraging providers to use healthcare ICT proven to reduce drugs costs such as computerized physician order entry (CPOE), which also reduces medical error rates, facilitates rational prescribing, and promotes best practices, hence reducing morbidities, and eventually would, costs. To be sure, the health insurance industry is not oblivious to its role in fostering healthcare ICT adoption. According to the Boston Globe, in its August 29, 2005, issue, Blue Cross and Blue Shield of Massachusetts announced its plans to launch a $50 million "experiment" to implement electronic health records (EHR) in three Massachusetts cities14. In Brockton, the biggest of the test sites, the plan was to convert paper-based patient records in a "diverse array" of hospitals, clinics, group practices, and independent physician offices to electronic format. The new EHR would make patient records available in real time at the point of care (POC), in disparate locations, even connected to physicians' offices, thereby enhancing quality, reducing morbidities, and saving lives. Some experts estimated that the cost of implementing an EHR system nationwide could be $230 billion, but would the overall long-term benefits of such investments not outweigh the costs? Would it not make a difference that the insurance industry continues to support healthcare ICT adoption? Could innovative ideas, such as the "must-have health insurance plan" recently proposed by Massachusetts Governor Mitt Romney, help pay the costs of the technologies, and assure returns in some of the investments eventually, of the insurance industry in facilitating healthcare ICT adoption[15]? Forty five million Americans do not have health insurance, but many of them can afford it, but simply choose to go without it, costing the country billions of dollars annually. The Governor wants such persons, and indeed, everyone in the state, to obtain one, and would not have anyone, particularly those who could afford to, having the public pay his or her healthcare expenses. Rather, individuals would have health insurance through their employers, or the government, and government would subsidize coverage for those who cannot afford even the $2.30 a week health insurance would cost in the state according to the Governor s plans. The recent proposal by the British health Secretary, Patricia Hewitt further highlights the significance many attribute to preventive health services and the promotion of healthy living. The Secretary unveiled Government's proposed medical "MoTs", plan, which offers all patients a medical check at five points in their lives, although this will not be compulsory nor would anyone receive sanctions for not taking the medical tests. Individuals will receive these examinations at birth; at 11 and 18years old; when they have their first child; and as they reach their fifties, with people told their chances of developing serious disease, such as cancer, heart disease, diabetes and other illnesses, and those most at risk allocated a personal trainer. The personal trainer will set goals for improving their diet and increasing the exercise they take, and help them to quit smoking and reduce drinking and stress. Many welcome the plan, which for example could reveal latent type II diabetes, giving affected persons the opportunity to receive prompt treatment before the disease damages the body, or even lead to deadly consequences. Furthermore, these checks could help reduce healthcare costs significantly by minimizing unnecessary hospitalizations, particularly combined with relevant ICT that could enable home-based monitoring and care delivery, cost-effectively. Here again, despite its critics warning against the plan s potential for abuse and the increased workloads it would place on GPs, its prospects for improving health and reducing healthcare costs are not contentious. What really do such developments in the health industry, the tendency of health and pensions benefits to drive major companies aground, government regulations mandating companies to contribute to state health insurance, the threat of an imminent pandemic, "must-have health insurance", the increasing mobility of labor, and many other recent events, mean for the future of health insurance? Do they themselves not mandate the health insurance industry to continue to support healthcare ICT adoption, and would such collaboration not benefit the industry in the long term? What do the facts that the US trade deficit, at a record $609 billion in 2004, the budget shortfall expected to reach an all-time high of $427 billion in the year to September, and the US, $7.2 trillion in debt portend for the future companies and of the health insurance industry? Is it any wonder that Bill Gates, who gave the Global plan to stop Tuberculosis (TB) $600million at the ongoing WEF in Davos, and Warren Buffet extended the dollar s three-year fall by another two? Could the US afford spiraling healthcare costs under these circumstances? Would help from the health insurance industry, particularly with little or nothing to lose, not make a difference to this state of the country's economy, if even only long-term? It may just be strategically prudent after all for the industry to recognize the intricate ties of its very survival to such intersectoral collaboration, and such ties indeed, are as potent in other countries.

References

1. Available at: http://news.yahoo.com/s/ap/20060123/ap_on_bi_ge/ford_uaw_text_1 Accessed on: January 23, 2006

2. Simon, G.E, Savarino, J., Operskalski, B., and Philip S. Wang Suicide Risk During Antidepressant Treatment. *Am. J Psychiatry* 2006 163: 41-47

3. Stolzenberg-Solomon, R.Z; Graubard, B.I; Chari, S, et. al. Insulin, Glucose, Insulin Resistance, and Pancreatic Cancer in Male Smokers. *JAMA.* 2005; 294: 2872-2878.

4. Survey of Household Spending. Statistics Canada, 2005

5. Available at:
http://www.kaisernetwork.org/daily_reports/rep_index.cfm?DR_ID=34988
Accessed on January 26, 2006

6. Haiman, C.A, Stram, D.O, Wilkens, et. al. Ethnic and Racial Differences in the Smoking-Related Risk of Lung Cancer *N Engl. J Med* 2006; 354: 333-342.

7. Available at:

http://www.halifaxlive.com/artman/publish/printer_heart_failure_062405_91223.shtml
Accessed on January 26, 2006

8. Available at:

http://www.kaisernetwork.org/daily_reports/rep_index.cfm?DR_ID=35016
Accessed on January 26, 2006

9. Alderman. AK, Wei, Y, and Birkmeyer, J.D. Use of Breast Reconstruction After Mastectomy Following the Women's Health and Cancer Rights Act. *JAMA.* 2006; 295: 387-388.

10. Alderman, AK, McMahon, L. Jr. and Wilkins, E.G. The national utilization of immediate and early delayed breast reconstruction and the effect of sociodemographic factors. Plast. Reconstr. Surg. 2003 Feb; 111(2):695-703

11. Available at:

http://www.kaisernetwork.org/daily_reports/rep_index.cfm?DR_ID=35049
Accessed on January 27, 2006

12. Available at:

http://www.americanprogress.org/site/pp.asp?c=biJRJ8OVF&b=1372037
Accessed on January 27, 2006

13. Available at:

http://secure.cihi.ca/cihiweb/dispPage.jsp?cw_page=media_07dec2005_e
Accessed on January 28, 2006

14. Available at: http://www.medicalnewstoday.com/medicalnews.php?newsid=29904
Accessed on January 28, 2006

15. Available at:
http://www.cbsnews.com/stories/2006/01/28/eveningnews/main1249052.shtml
Accessed on January 28, 2006

16. Available at:
http://www.telegraph.co.uk/news/main.jhtml?xml=/news/2006/01/28/uhealth.xml&

sSheet=/portal/2006/01/28/ixportaltop.html
Accessed on January 28, 2006

ICT and the New Health Insurance Paradigm

T he health insurance industry is heading for a major paradigm shift. The convergence of economic, health, and technology factors is creating a new reality that would inevitably result in a change in mindset and approaches to doing business in the health insurance industry. These factors are not unique to any country although there are variations in the specificities of particular factors, and others have significant local flavors. That health is a major national strategic resource is increasingly clear, as indeed, is the need for global health initiatives in order to avert catastrophic global pandemics, but also the spillover effects of national health burdens across the globe. To underscore this point, the UN Development Program (UNDP) has drawn up a visionary proposal, already endorsed by a number of world figures including Gordon Brown, the British Chancellor of the Exchequer, and Joseph Stiglitz, the 2001 Economics Nobel Laureate, who won the prize along with two other Americans G. Akerlof, and A. Michael. The trio won the award for their analyses of markets with asymmetric information. Incidentally, it was Professor Stiglitz, a former chief economist at the World Bank, who said at a press conference in Columbia, USA after the announcement of his award, Market economies are characterized by a high degree of imperfections. Older models assumed perfect information, but even small degrees of information imperfections can have large economic consequences. Our models took into account asymmetries of information, which is another way of saying Some people know more than others. We well come back to the significance of this statement for the inevitable changes in the operations of the health insurance industry a little later. The UNDP proposal calls for an admission that the concept of the nation-state is outmoded in a modern globalized world in which it is counterintuitive to jettison rather than harness financial markets. It also called for unlocking $7 trillion (£ 3.9trn) of previously untapped wealth and cooperation between countries via six specific financial tools, in order to end the most potent threats to life on earth, namely, global warming, health pandemics, poverty, and armed conflict. Analysts believe that this proposal, revealed at the recent weeklong World Economic Forum (WEF) conference that ended in Davos, Switzerland on January 29, 2006, if endorsed by countries, would mandate them to account for the cost of failed policies, and utilize the money saved proactively, in crisis prevention. The benefits derivable would far outweigh the costs of securing money from the financial markets up front for risk management and crisis prevention, experts insist. An analysis of the UNDP proposal in the context of the benefits of globalization, which some claim have only so far favored multinationals, is apt, and should make the reasoning behind the goal of the organization of extending the largesse of globalization to society's poor not far to seek, as indeed, the tie this has to the health insurance industry. In particular, the idea of tackling global warning, poverty and disease, based on collaborating with the global markets to facilitate risk sharing, has a strong bearing on the health insurance industry. Among the schemes already proposed is a pilot international finance facility (IFF) to front load $4bn of cash for vaccines by borrowing money against pledges of future government aid, a scheme the UK, France, Italy, Spain, Sweden and the Bill and Melinda Gates Foundation back. The scheme emanated from a proposal for a larger scheme to double the total annual aid budget to $100bn, by Gordon Brown, the British Chancellor of the Exchequer. The six schemes the UNDP proposed to harness the power of the markets and their net gains are reducing greenhouse gas emissions through pollution permit trading with a net gain of $3.64trn, and cutting poor countries borrowing costs by securing the debts against the income from stable parts of their economies with a net gain of $2.90trn. The others are reducing government debt costs by linking payments to the country's economic output with a net gain of $600bn, an enlarged version of the vaccine scheme; net gain (including benefits of lower mortality) of $47bn, and using the vast flow of money from migrants back to their home country to guarantee, net gain $31bn. The sixth involves agencies underwriting loans to market investors to lower interest rates, net gain $22bn. The essence of these proposals is the need for collective action to ensure the prosperity and security of the global economy in tandem with equity both within and across countries, the panacea for genuine sustainable economic development. These measures are clearly going to cause schisms in local, national, and global markets whose effect on the health insurance industry it could simply not wish away. How for example, would such massive investments in vaccines not have a positive effect on peoples' health? Consider, for example, that Tamiflu conceivably prevented the catastrophic consequences that would have otherwise occurred in a hypothetical scenario in which there was an outbreak of avian flu pandemic. How much would the health insurance industry have saved in averted claims? What would have been the net gain in human and economic terms to a country's economy that its factories are still operational, and not shut down because people were too ill to come to work? What would the insurance industry lose supporting such schemes to prevent diseases before they start, even in a collective global effort? How would the operations of the industry shift to accommodate the new focus on disease prevention that many countries now embrace? The UK for example recently unveiled its plans to make National Health Service (NHS) care more accessible by moving it into the community in an initiative that the Health Secretary described as "a major strategic shift". The plan would also mean treating fewer patients in hospitals, and opening the GP market to private and voluntary sector to make up for the shortage of healthcare professionals in some areas. These changes are going to affect the health insurance industry in the U.K in profound ways. With one out of every four trusts in the U.K finishing 2005 in deficit, and hospitals forced to close wards, freeze recruitment and holdup operations to balance their accounts, the U.K government believes that this plan would not only help to ensure equitable health service provision, but also reduce unnecessary hospitalizations and overall, health costs. The specific measures in the plan include, push for a new generation of community hospitals, providing diagnostics, minor surgery, intermediate care and basic primary care, and encouraging family doctors to open for longer and set up specialist clinics for conditions such as diabetes and ear, nose and throat treatment. Others are incorporating social workers more into the NHS by placing them alongside GPs in surgeries and care campuses and through closer co-operation between councils and NHS trusts, and the introduction of Health MoTs, which give patients the option of periodic health checkups to see if they are at risk of developing conditions such as heart disease and diabetes. The plan also includes encouraging private and voluntary sectors involvement in NHS community market, and pushing for high street stores such as Boots and Tesco to host health clinics. Largely restricted to hospital operations, the private sector have rarely ventured outside this domain in the NHS until now, when government wants to see health firms and voluntary organizations running GP practices, as well as nurses, pharmacists and other health professionals, such as physiotherapists given more duties. The plan is already creating divisions, particularly with regard the involvement of the private sector, a perennial contentious issue in health financing in the UK, with the

British Medical Association (BMA) for example, which, along with the Royal College of General Practitioners (RCGP), endorsed the plan, advocating for giving NHS providers priority over private firms. Expectedly, the BMA is also concerned about where the estimated 10,000 GPs, one third of the total, needed to fill gaps in care and to replace retiring doctors in the years ahead would come from. While there is no disputing the need to recruit more GPs into the NHS, the implementation of appropriate healthcare ICT could help minimize the adverse effects of this shortage of healthcare professionals, both in the short-and long-terms. A quick example is incorporating the use of home medical evaluation and monitoring healthcare ICT into the plan. These devices, in conjunction with extended telehealth services could result in substantial costs reduction, while ensuring the provision of qualitative services simultaneously. An important aspect of the plan is the continuity of care, which would require the ability of healthcare providers in the community to access patients' health records readily and in real time at the point of care (POC). This demands the implementation of sophisticated electronic health records (EHR), a sine qua non for the proposed plan to succeed. It is clear that health insurers in the UK would have to be an integral part of this extended digitalization of patients records if they were to participate effectively in the new programs. Such firms would have to start rethinking their healthcare ICT strategy, and planning not just on implementing newer cutting-edge technologies that would facilitate data and information communication and sharing between them, the GPs, and other healthcare providers, but also those that would modify and streamline their administrative processes to accommodate the changes that their more extensive operations would demand. To reassure those who worry about funding the plan, the UK government has indicated that funding for most of the proposed measures would be via money already promised the health service, in effect the percentage of the NHS budget spent on community NHS services increasing only by 5%, to a third, in keeping with OECD standards. Nonetheless, private insurers would need to contribute to the more widespread use of healthcare ICT particularly now that they are venturing outside their previous hospital domain into the community, where ICT diffusion is not as pervasive. Indeed, and for the smoother running of their own operations, private insurers would have to start considering even providing GPs with incentives to encourage them to implement healthcare ICT, which GPs would need anyway, also to facilitate the increasing management tasks they would have to perform in this new dispensation. Insurers would also need to play an increasing role in disease prevention, and in promoting healthy living, both of which would not only help reduce rates of illnesses, but would also reduce needless hospitalizations, and reduce health costs, buoying bottom line. This new plan heralds a new era of private sector involvement in healthcare delivery in the U.K and underscores the emerging paradigm shift in health insurance, which clearly would transcend national boundaries. To illustrate this point, there are reports that a major US health firm is to take over GP services in Derbyshire, U.K., whose local health chiefs recently chose the European arm of United Health, to run two practices. UnitedHealth Europe purchases healthcare on behalf of governments and major employers for around 55 million patients, and contracts with over 4000 hospitals and 400 000 doctors. Indeed, private firms would conduct one in 10 non-emergency operations by 2008. North Eastern Derbyshire Primary Care Trust chose UnitedHealth Europe from a shortlist of six bids. Boots, Bupa, Care UK, Netcare, BMI, UnitedHealth, Nuffield, Alliance Medical, and a host of other firms would likely become providers to the NHS, in a variety of settings, the high street, in the new surgeries, diagnostic centers, and community centers, and some, commissioners of care for the NHS, operating on contract to primary care trusts. With entry barriers minimal, competition in the growing market would increase as new entrants including groupings of NHS and entrepreneurial GPs enter the scene. As services migrate into the community, challenges face traditional hospitals ahead, which would require appropriate adjustments, including takeovers, and mergers, and some might even have to cease operations, all these no doubt with consequences for the insurance industry. The issue of maintenance of standards and the quality of care delivery would be clearly on the agenda of all stakeholders, including consumer advocacy groups. The klieg lights would also be on the insurance industry, which would need to ensure the continuity of high standards and qualitative service provision in their jurisdictions, the achievement of which goals would no doubt require the right attitude toward healthcare ICT implementation, among others. The private finance initiative (PFI) would need to adjust, not with about £ 5bn spent on PFI hospitals, £ 6bn, out to tender and the strategic outline cases approved worth a further £ 6bn. Government's intention to re-evaluate and approve only major capital procurement forthwith that are compatible with its commitment to shift to community services underlines its seriousness about that commitment. Indeed, the Health Secretary indicated that after this reevaluation, estimates of approvable PFI programs, £ 7bn to £ 9bn, would still be larger that those already built or under construction, although a 25 to 40 per cent decrease on future plans. Despite these changes in healthcare delivery in the UK, the answer to the question of whether NHS hospitals and foundation trusts would expand into primary and community care remains uncertain, an answer that private insurers anticipate with understandable apprehension. From the 1984, Griffiths Report on the NHS that asked that GPs have more autonomy to build community services, to the idea of GP fundholding, with GPs given their own budgets, scrapped in 1997, reintroduced as practice-based commissioning in 2004. These followed by the scrapping of much of the internal market idea, transformed into the 300 primary care trusts that exist today, and now the concept of GP contract started in 2004 that gives GPs monetary incentives for providing specialist services, all suggest that the idea of shifting care to the community has a fairly long history. Incidentally, the idea of GP contract fist started in 1990 when GPs got extra money for working in health promotion clinics. Unlike in the past, however, when reforms either pitch doctor against doctor, as some argue the idea of GP fundholding did, or not all embraced the reforms, the NHS seems united in support for this new plan.

Primary care reforms are also ongoing in other countries, including Canada. Projections from recent estimates of Canada's gross domestic product (GDP) put the ratio of health expenditure to GDP at 10.1% in 2004. Based on 2002 comparative figures, the latest available, Canada at 9.6% ranks fourth among G8 countries in total health expenditure as a percentage of GDP, after the United States (14.6%), Germany (10.9%) and France (9.7%), with the UK, Italy, Japan and Russia, next in that order. Most of the healthcare budget in Canada goes into funding for hospitals and drugs, $38.9 billion in 2004, or just less than 30% of total health expenditure, but there is increasing emphasis on primary health care and population health. In 2000, Canada's First Ministers greed that, "improvements to primary health care are crucial to the renewal of health services". In response to this agreement, the Government of Canada established the $800 million Primary Health Care Transition Fund (PHCTF), which over a six-year period (2000-2006), would go into supporting provinces and territories in their efforts to reform the primary health care system, specifically the transitional costs needed to introduce new approaches to primary health care delivery. There is also much interest in reforming the healthcare system at the secondary and tertiary levels, although the focus is primarily on the first tier of health services delivery. The Ten-Year Plan to Strengthen Health Care signed on September 16, 2004, by the Prime Minister and all Premiers and Territorial Leaders addresses the country's priorities for sustaining and renewing the health care system, and provides $41 billion over ten years to put into operating the reforms. As in the UK and elsewhere, family physicians are crucial to Canada's primary health care and population health goals, being in the main, the first contact in the pathway to healthcare, and often, the last. More than half of Canadian physicians are family physicians. 61% of Canadian family doctors and 48% of its specialists are in group-rather than solo- practices. Rising healthcare costs and physician shortage/ mal-distribution keep physician-resource policy issues firmly on the health agenda, well after the Kilshaw report (1995), and all those before it including the Barer/ Stoddart report (1991.) The direction of consensus of subsequent reports for physician payments, a key issue in these reports, seems to be toward capitation or a blended payment system with extra compensation for spending more time with patients and conducting preventive health programs. Many believe that this will facilitate Canada's realization of its goals of primary care reform including the promotion of equitable, accessible, and quality care, sustainable and effective preventive care, more accountability, improved distribution of physicians, and health costs that are more predictable. Some may contend that the failed Ontario's HSO program is evidence that capitation is suspect, others, highlight its robust results in some European countries such as Norway, but all would probably agree that fee-for-service is not cost-effective and is hampering primary care reform in the country. There is also consensus that how doctors get paid under primary care reform will influence expectations of how they do their job; that fee-for-service may be escalating costs due to doctors providing more services than necessary; and that other factors beside remuneration influence the quality of service delivery by doctors such as job satisfaction. In response to the reports on physician resource and related policy issues, including the 1997 National Forum on Health report, the federal government has been infusing funds via the $150 million Health Transition Fund and later via the $800 million Primary Health Care Transition Fund into several primary care pilot projects since 1997/ 98. However, not a few believe that these projects have added little if any reform to the primary care system, and that a graded rather than a big-bang approach to primary care reform will work better, and policy makers seem to be listening. The Romanow Commission (2002) gave credence to this incremental approach, criticizing the ad-hoc, short-term, and piece meal, nature of funding for the pilot projects without exploiting their potential for overhauling the entire healthcare system. The Commission argued in its 2002 report for targeted funding to stimulate a major breakthrough in implementing primary healthcare reform and revamping the healthcare system, the Health Council of Canada, which made certain recommendations, including accelerating the introduction of IT, spearheading and mobilizing these reform activities. In making its recommendations, the Council, which also acknowledged the difficulty with physicians relinquishing solo practices for group practices, and with multidisciplinary teams providing comprehensive 24/ 7 year-round practices, underscored the recognition by policy makers of the significant role of ICT in healthcare delivery. Every province and territory wants to meet the agreed target of half of Canadians having round the clock, year-round access to multidisciplinary teams by 2011. There is therefore substantial injection of funds into efforts to achieve this goal, accelerating the pace and nature of primary care reform in the country at the provincial/ territorial, and the federal levels. Indeed, the Federal government s $16 billion Health Reform Fund of 2003 also included funds for home and catastrophic drug expenses, and transitioned into the Canada Health Transfer fund in 2004, a reflection of the shift in approach from targeted time-limited primary care funding to continuing funding for a variety of initiatives with national goals, and performance appraisals. Canada s Medicare is primarily a public health system, but with increasing private input. It is unclear, however, how much longer it would take a parallel private health system to evolve fully in the country considering the recent Supreme Court decision in Quebec giving its citizens the right to seek private health care. ICT spending constituted less than 2% of Canada s overall healthcare spending in 2003 but that also is changing, and would likely increase with more private sector involvement in healthcare delivery in the country. The Office of Health and the Information Highway announced a new program intended to support the application of innovative technology in healthcare delivery as far back as 2000. The Canada Health Infostructure Partnerships

Program (CHIPP), which replaced the Health Infostructure Support Program (HISP), emphasized large implementation models and collaboration across jurisdictions. It offers a two-year, shared-cost incentive to promote ICT implementation. CHIPP specifically aimed to support ICT-enabled healthcare delivery applications in the areas of telehealth, and EHR. The intention to facilitate data and information accessibility and sharing remains as germane to high quality healthcare delivery today, as it was back then. Indeed, increasing healthcare ICT utilization in health services delivery at all levels of care in Canada is evident. For example, in its 2004 budget, the Federal government gave the Canadian Health Infostructure Initiative (CHI) an additional $100 million to foster the development and implementation of a pan-Canadian health surveillance system with a view to integrating present disease-based surveillance systems, and to support the management of infectious disease prevention and protection activities. Indeed, the Federal government has given CHI $1.2 billion since 2001 to work with provinces and territories to develop Pan-Canadian eHealth solutions for electronic health records (EHR), telehealth and health surveillance. Both the public and private sectors, fund Canada's health system. However, the provinces and territories remain responsible for administering and delivering health care services, guided by the provisions of the Canada Health Act. Estimates for total health expenditure, in current dollars, for 2002 were $114.0 billion, in 2003, $123.0 billion, and in 2004, $130.3 billion, and for total health expenditure per capita in 2002, $3,635, in 2003, $3,885, and in 2004, were $4,078, the 2004 forecast a 12.2% increase from the 2002 amount. Analysts predict that the total Canadian ICT market would be almost $75-billion in 2006, increasing by another $5-billion in two years. Health insurers cannot afford to ignore developments in the ICT industry as well. Progress with multicore servers and in novel, multifunctional microprocessors, with expected reduction in power usage, hence costs, would doubtless redefine data storage and management approaches even in the health insurance industry. Software as a service (SAAS), essentially rental software, is also gaining increasing currency, especially in customer relations management and sales-force automation. Picture archiving and communication systems (PACS), electronic health records (EHR) technologies, computerized physician order entry (CPOE) systems, and a variety of communication and information sharing technologies, including short-messaging services (SMS), and multimedia messaging services (MMS), and mobile TV via IP technology, would become increasingly adopted in the health industry, which would impact the healthcare ICT strategy of insurance firms. Health insurance firms like the health industry, would need to invest in wireless and mobile technologies, which would be increasingly important for real time information access. Both industries would face the challenge as does the ICT industry of issues relating to standards and interoperability, for example deciding which of the main competing novel digital video disc formats, Sony's Blu-ray or HD DVD, of Intel, Toshiba and Microsoft, to adopt. Health ICT spending varies across the country, but there is appreciation of the role ICT would play in achieving the agreed primary care reform goals across board. Let us illustrate what typically happens in all Canadian provinces and territories, albeit to varying degrees, with the example of Alberta. The province allocated $2.6 million from its Telehealth Clinical Services Grant Fund to twenty-one new telehealth initiatives in the province in 2005. The funds are for telehealth initiatives in six health regions, the Alberta Mental Health Board, and the Alberta Cancer Board. The provision of quality patient care and access to services feature prominently in the province s healthcare plans, on which it spent a total of $7.4 billion in 2003/ 04, an increase of $529.6 million (7.7 per cent) over 2002/ 2003. Of this amount, the province spent $29.0 million on health reform and renewal initiatives such as a 24-hour telephone information services (Health Link Alberta), and on implementing its electronic health record. The province has also established a $66 million Alberta Physician Office System Program in collaboration with the Alberta Medical Association. Every physician in the province is now eligible to $7,700 in each of four years to install, undergo training in, and start to use electronic medical records (EMR) in his/ her practice, and over half its doctors have responded. The EMRs in doctors' offices integrate with the provincial EHR, no doubt an enabling environment for seamless communication and information sharing from which private insurance would benefit hooked with, and the reason the health insurance industry should want to collaborate with not just the Alberta government, but others in encouraging healthcare ICT diffusion among healthcare providers. It is clearly in the interest of all stakeholders, including the industry to operate in a fully digitalized and modern healthcare system. The US government awarded over US$18 million contracts in November 2005 alone to build four prototypes for its national health information network. Some, for example the Center for Health

Transformation, founded by Newt Gingrich, former US House Speaker, in a report released on November 28, 2005, are calling for even more ICT spending. Specifically the Center asked that the US dedicates 1% of federal discretionary spending, or about $7 billion annually, to health ICT, which the organization regards as critical to reducing medical errors and increasing disaster preparedness. The country awarded three contracts in October 2005, amounting to US$17.5 to expand the use of EHR and develop standards for EHR product regulation, and a US$3.3 million contract to the American National Standards Institute to develop software standards that would facilitate patient information sharing among providers. The third was a US$2.7 million contract awarded to the Certification Commission for Health Information Technology to develop standards for EHR products certification. The U.S also awarded a US$11.5 million contract to the Health Information Security and Privacy Collaboration to establish health care privacy regulations, and continues to award even more healthcare ICT contracts in its bid to facilitate increased healthcare ICT diffusion. Implementation cost is a key barrier to ICT adoption in the health industry, particularly in physician practices, and in small and rural hospitals, according to a recent survey released in October 2005, by the American Hospital Association. The same pattern of increasing investment in healthcare ICT to back-up healthcare reforms, particularly at the primary healthcare level is evident in other developed countries such as Australia and New Zealand, in the South hemisphere and many European countries in the North. Is it farfetched then to conjecture that the health insurance industry would have to follow suit in not just implementing cutting-edge ICT that would enable it participate successfully in the collaborative effort to improve healthcare delivery, to make it more accessible, and cost-effective, but also preventing diseases and promoting healthy living? How much appreciation of the health and technology issues involved does the health insurance industry need to have in order to tune-in with new developments in the health industry and travel in the direction that the industry heads, and is this not urgent? Does it not call for a novel approach to doing business by the health insurance industry? Would this not in fact be in the industry's best interest overall?

Disease prevention is the major thrust of the UNDP proposal mentioned earlier. One key approach to disease prevention is eliminating information asymmetry. By providing patients with current and accurate information on health issues for example, it is likely that they would know what measures to take to prevent them contracting disease. For example, someone that knows that he or she could contract Hepatitis A via the fecal-oral route and that simple hand washing after using the bathroom could prevent this deadly infection, would likely conform to this life-saving practice. This simple health education could save many lives and reduce illness and hospitalization rates, saving significant health costs. The involvement of a health insurance firm in rectifying such information asymmetry could also help reduce actuarial risk, and increase its profitability. Healthcare ICT could facilitate health education of this sort with benefits accruing to all stakeholders. Six percent of babies born worldwide annually, almost 8 million, have serious birth defects, about 95% of them born in middle and low-income countries, according to the March of Dimes agency, which recently conducted the first inclusive global analysis of the problem based on facts gathered from 193 countries around the world. 3.3 million Children under the age of 5 years, die every year due to these problems, an estimated 3.2 million of those who survive typically permanently mentally and physically disabled. Thousands more children are born with serious birth defects linked to exposure in the womb to alcohol, or infections such as rubella or syphilis, although not included in the current report. The report noted the chances of reducing morbidity and mortality due to genetic birth defects by as much as 70% by such simple measures as giving pregnant women folic acid supplements, which could reduce the risk of spina bifida. There is no doubt also about the role that healthcare ICT could play in educating pregnant women about the risks to their babies of drinking alcohol during pregnancy. Indeed, these facts make the development of basic services such as family planning, and adequate nutrition for pregnant mothers and children, and basic screening and preventive services, as already exist in developed countries, in middle-income countries, slightly different approaches, no doubt, crucial. Birth defects occur in all countries of the world and for different reasons, with resultant differential effects on health services utilization, facts that not only healthcare providers, but also health insurers want to know that are critical for service planning and resource allocation to the former, and competitive pricing for the latter. Indeed, it is increasingly important for the health insurance industry to appreciate the details of developments in the health industry in order to operate successfully there. Take for example, the concept of disease management. Some would fret over the gracelessness of this not-entirely-novel term, which the healthcare industry applies to describe efforts to monitor the medical problems of chronically ill patients while simultaneously assisting them with treatment compliance. The anticipated claims reduction with disease-management programs, which some also criticize as somewhat expensive, did not materialize at least as much as the health insurance industry hoped that it would. However, times have changed, and there are now cost-effective healthcare ICT that, if deployed appropriately to address particular issues and improve specific processes would likely yield the desired medical and pecuniary results. Some countries, for example, Germany, are actually compensating insurers for some of the cost of implementing these cutting-edge technologies, an example of the collaborative endeavors that is becoming more pervasive in contemporary healthcare delivery.

The European Commission (EU) has identified healthcare as a major strategic target area for improvement, and healthcare ICT a major resource in achieving this goal. It has also recognized that the adoption of IT in healthcare is not only a European but also a global initiative and it is very keen to promote knowledge sharing between industry, government and the research community. It also encourages the exchange of experiences regarding the current state of e-adoption at sectoral, national, regional, and international levels, including facilitating access to the European Research Area (ERA) by interested researchers worldwide. Several European countries are taking their cue from this positive leadership position of the EU and investing substantially in healthcare ICT. France for example, is likely going to invest substantially on healthcare ICT in the near future, particularly clinical systems, such as CPOE and EHR, considering its increased interest in ensuring patient safety, analysts predicting the growth of healthcare ICT market from the current $726m per annum spending to $1,034m by 2008, a 30% increase. As is happening in the UK, Canada, and elsewhere, France is also strengthening its primary care services hence the expectation of increased investments on integrated solutions that would seamlessly connect disparate service areas. The country s new activity-based funding system, commenced in 2004, continues to influence the operations of all aspects of healthcare delivery in France, hospitals forced to rationalize services and invest more on healthcare ICT in order to ensure accurate recording of patient activity so that they would receive the proper reimbursement. The two-pronged strategic requirement for healthcare ICT in France is setting the pace for all stakeholders in the health system, and that government expectedly wants its investments to yield returns further places the onus on other stakeholders to align with government s strategic goals. Despite faced with crippling budget deficits, the French government continues to invest in healthcare ICT, albeit at a slower pace than it might otherwise wish, against the backdrop of its strong commitments to improving the quality of healthcare delivery to its peoples. The EU regulations mandating placement of the bigger tenders in the Official Journal of the European Union, is likely to open the healthcare industry to more private sector interests, increasing competition, possibly reducing costs. With France pursuing its goal of an integrated national health IT plan apace, the private sector could hope to find a buoyant market, but one in which competition is likely to be very stiff, although as in most other markets, there are other issues for examples those of standards and interoperability that beset the French healthcare ICT milieu. Healthcare ICT spending is increasing in other European countries. Indeed, experts predict that total IT spending in the Western European healthcare sector would increase from $7bn (£ 3.9bn) in 2004 to $10bn (£ 5.6bn) in 2009. In Sweden, the universal social policy persists but has been undergoing reforms in recent times, the country under economic strain increasingly burdened by high benefit rates, resulting in reductions in some benefits, or restrictions placed on them. In Sweden, county councils and municipalities are responsible for organizing healthcare delivery, primary care the basis of health and medical care. Healthcare remains financed through tax revenues, although patients still pay for certain services, and more the more complex, the country s high-cost protection scheme pegging the upper limit in any one-year period. The percentage of private care providers in publicly financed health and medical care hiked in the 1990s, with staff or user cooperatives, non-profit organizations, private enterprises, and joint-stock companies in agreements with county councils to deliver health services, most located in primary care, operating health centers. Private businesses manage some hospitals, and private care providers account for 10% of total health care costs. Private care where the patients pay all costs of care, and private health insurance, constitute small portions of Sweden s health system, although the number private health insurance policies is progressively on the rise, 127 000 individual policies and 77 000 group policies in 2003[2]. It is likely that the private health insurance scene in Sweden would continue to evolve, although there are signs of continuing government control of health matters in the country. For example, government s proposals in the Government Bill ˙Forms of operation for publicly financed hospitals˙ (2004/ 05:145) to amend the Health and Medical Services Act (1982:763), expected to come into force on January 01, 2006. This proposal essentially seeks to mandate the county councils to run at least one hospital themselves within their own area, and disallow them to entrust the operation of regional hospitals or regional clinics to any other party. The proposal also requests county councils to stipulate in the contract, if they transferred the operation of other hospitals to another party, that the operations may run for profit making for the contractor and that the financing of the care would be exclusively with public funds and care fees. Nonetheless, it is also clear that the country acknowledges the need for private health insurance. In fact, it already exists in a number of forms, for example, the patient insurance scheme, set up to compensate a patient injured in connection with treatment or similar healthcare measure, with all healthcare providers mandated by law to take out patient insurance, which though does not cover injuries caused by pharmaceutical products. These latter injuries, the pharmaceutical insurance cover, a voluntary, unregulated, collective insurance provided by members of the Swedish Pharmaceutical Insurance Association, either in their position as Swedish manufacturers or as importers of pharmaceuticals manufactured overseas. To buttress the point that private health insurance might become even more widespread in Sweden, the government via its Ministry of Health and Social Affairs, established a Commission on Profit or Not-for-Profit in the Swedish Health System over ten years ago. The country is also not oblivious to its obligations in the EU and other global organizations, such as the OECD and the World health organization (WHO) and acknowledges that these commitments would likely influence the direction its healthcare goes, another example of the increasing acceptance of the need for collaboration at all levels that developments in today's health scene demand. Issues such as mobility of individuals, and of labor, and capital do influence health policy, and by extension, health insurance. Sweden is no exception with regard to these important aspects of contemporary global economy. Whether inspired by Bismarck or by Beveridge, as are the German, Swiss, and French health systems by the former, and the British, Spanish, the Scandinavian countries by the latter, Western Europe s health, and welfare systems are undergoing changes that have far-reaching implications for health insurance, driven by a variety of health and non-health factors, including significantly, healthcare ICT. Many of these changes are in synchrony with developments in both the health and insurance industries in other developed countries, although they are not all always moving along the path of change in tandem. An example of disparities in approach is the issue of the legally blind being legally authorized to drive with bioptic glasses, hundreds of them already doing so in California, and in many states in the US, Canada and Australia giving approval, as opposed to the UK and other European countries. Is it at all open to doubt the effect that this policy, which enables individuals who would otherwise have been housebound able to go wherever they wish, using miniaturized telescopic lenses attached to their glasses making vision much clearer, would have on actuarial risk assessment, insurance policies and pricing?

In the US provider and payer, healthcare ICT spending was roughly $26 billion in 2004 expected to increase to over $34 billion by 2008, with a CAGR of 7%, payer spending in 2008, $7.5 billion, and provider spending, $26.7 billion the same year. Services would constitute most of the revenue in the payer segment, and would increase from $2.5 billion to $3.5 billion between 2004 and 2008, over 40% of the market, superior technology-based services, for example, claims outsourcing the chief driver. Hospitals would continue to consume most of healthcare ICT funds in the provider domain, about 57% of the market, increasing from $11.7 billion to $15 billion during the same period. As with health systems everywhere, that in the U.S has its own problems. Indeed, on January 30, 2006, the American College of Physicians released a statement warning of the imminent collapse of the country's primary care system, barring immediate reforms₁. The College lamented, "Very few young physicians are going into primary care, and those already in practice are under such stress that they are looking for an exit strategy," with 35% of doctors in the US over 55 years old, the prospects of many retiring soon are very real. What's more, according to the College, in 2003, only 27% of third year internal medicine residents planned to practice internal medicine, the others contemplating more lucrative specialties. This is not surprising because primary care physicians, who constitute the first doctors most people, see when they are ill, and essentially the pillar of healthcare in any society, are at the bottom of the list of all medical specialties in median income compensation. The College considers the fall in

Medicare reimbursement a key issue in the shortage of primary care doctors in the US. Other problems include difficulties in juggling patients, soaring bills, and insurers policies that encourage rushed office visits, according to the College, which suggested new ways of paying doctors that would enable primary care doctors focus on patient's care and patients more responsibility for monitoring their own health and appointments scheduling, both that would require significant healthcare ICT input. The suggestion seems to attempt to address the long-standing complaint by doctors in the country that reimbursement policies of both Medicare and private insurers reward a "just-in-time" approach, instead of preventive care, which they argue reduces health costs and promotes health. Here again, the health insurance industry could expect to have to deal with remuneration issues of this sort in the years ahead. According to the College, "Medicare will pay tens of thousands of dollars ... for a limb amputation on a diabetic patient, but virtually nothing to the primary care physician for keeping the patient's diabetes under control." This situation certainly conflicts with the direction in which healthcare delivery in tending toward, and from which incidentally the health insurance would benefit on the aggregate, even if not right away. The College also suggested innovations such as e-mail consultation on minor and routine matters, which would free up costly office visit time for when necessary, with of course doctors recompensed for such consultations. There is no doubt that non-conventional modes of consultation are becoming increasingly common, and would likely become more widespread, particularly with progress in such technologies as SMS and MMS. Health insurers would have to examine ways of reimbursing doctors for such consultations, and ensuring that neither patients nor doctors abuse the process. This is another example of the need for insurance companies to pay close attention to their ICT strategy, as monitoring and reimbursing some of the new consultation and treatment modalities effectively and efficiently is likely to pose significant challenges. Considering that there is research evidence of the effectiveness of some of these new, technology-based approaches, for example telephone cognitive therapy and many more would turn out to be also effective, it would be difficult for insurance companies to ignore them. The increasing acceptance of consumer-driven healthcare is also going to influence the insurance industry as patients become more involved in decision making regarding their health issues, including treatment options. With many doctors actually prepared to stop taking

Medicare patients, insurers have a major issue to deal with. Indeed, the insurance industry cannot ignore issues regarding the immediate, short-and long-term resource requirements of the health system, and this applies to all countries. In the UK, for example, the Wanless report, ¨Securing Our Future Health: Taking A Long-Term View,¨ is the first ever evidence-based assessment of the long-term resource requirements for the NHS. In March 2001, the Chancellor of the Exchequer requested Sir Derek Wanless, former Natwest bank chief executive, to review the drivers of health care expenditure in the UK and their likely effect on the resources needed for the health service over the next 20 years. In its final report, published in 2002, The Review, among others, concluded that the UK must expect to devote a considerably larger share of its national income to health care over the next 20 years if it were to meet peoples expectations and the costs of technological innovation. The Review considered this necessary for Britain to catch up with the standards of care seen in other countries and to deliver a wide-ranging, high quality service for the public and individual patients, and recommended continuing funding of the health service through general taxation, which it considered the most cost effective and fairest system for the future. The Review indeed, felt that there is no evidence that any alternative financing method to the UK's NHS would deliver a given quality of healthcare at a lower cost to the economy¨, and that ¨other systems seem likely to prove more costly. Nor do alternative balances of funding appear to offer scope to increase equity.¨ Sir Wanless stressed the need for more investment in information technology in order to improve efficiency of healthcare delivery and reduce costs. His call for¨ radical changes in the skill mix of the workforce¨, which implies the need to extend the role of nurses, for example, underscores the urgency of the need to address the perennial shortage of healthcare professionals, and the role that healthcare ICT could play in ameliorating this problem, and facilitating the delivery of qualitative health services. Sir Wanless' suggestion that ¨more self-care by patients¨ could help to reduce financial pressure on the health service, also highlights the important role healthcare ICT would play in future health services delivery in the UK, with patients encouraged to stay at home and take care of themselves, rather than visit their GP or local hospital. This is also an indication of the shift in thinking toward community health services mentioned earlier, and a measure of the increasing importance of the idea of population health with its mandatory need for primary care reforms, with emphasis on providing and funding health services based on the population s needs, reducing the costs of funding services after disease has occurred. Besides the need for a realistic resource requirements analysis, and for developing appropriate recruitment and retention solutions, health systems would have to place increasing emphasis on population health, disease prevention, and health promotion. They would also need to encourage multidisciplinary approaches to decision-making, and community participation in health issues. Healthcare ICT would feature significantly in these measures and in achieving the goals set out in various initiatives including improving accessibility, affordability and the quality of health services, and facilitating standardization, and interoperability of information systems within and in disparate healthcare locations. New Zealand for example has been able to integrate information from a variety of sources into an accurate depiction of the individual patient s state of health, which facilitates the provision of qualitative, patient-focused care with its unique identifier system, the National Health Index (NHI.) The idea of a unique identifier is even more important in an increasingly mobile world. With individuals, not only changing jobs rapidly, which often entails changing locations, with the chances of seeking primary, secondary, even tertiary health services in these new locations, what would be the consequences of having multiple identifiers for the same individual? Could this not prevent or slow timely access to critical health information, for which some criticize Australia s Medicare number system? How would a health insurance company fare competitively if not integrated into a health information system based on unique identifiers? Software developers have used the NHI as a platform for a variety of projects, for examples nationwide health data networks that link hospitals, labs, radiology services and GPs to point-of-care (POC), and Internet technologies for healthcare providers. The NHI has also inspired the building of clinical systems for GPs, and electronic billing processing systems, and ICT diffusion among healthcare providers in general, some studies indicating that 99% of New Zealand GPs have implemented a software application for practice management, which 71.8% of them use for clinical notes storage in electronic formats. The country also has the world s first practice management system for ophthalmologists that integrates and interfaces with third party ophthalmology applications, another indication of its acknowledgement of the value of healthcare ICT in improving health outcomes.

The future of private health insurance in countries such as the UK, Canada, Australia, and New Zealand is somewhat fluid with issues such as finance, access, ownership, and management, posing major challenges. In Australia for example, whether affluent people should take up private health insurance, rebates/ incentives for private health insurance, and whether those with private health insurance should still be able to access the public health systems, remain thorny issues. Privately insured persons currently also receive a Private Health Insurance Rebate, which translates to at least 30% of their insurance premiums, incentives that some believe would encourage people to purchase private health insurance and ease the burden on the public systems, which often has long hospital wait lists. However, others think it unnecessary and better spent to improve the public health systems. Some even say such incentives only encourage people, and roughly a third of Australians do, to keep private health insurance, while still using public health services when more convenient. In fact, the number of Australians that have private health insurance is increasing with the introduction of Lifetime Health Cover, which makes purchasing private hospital insurance later in life more expensive, and tax incentives to take out private cover, such as the Medicare Levy Surcharge, an additional 1% to the 1.5% medical levy. Coupled with the incentive of shorter wait lists, ability to choose hospital and/ or doctor, and have private rooms, which the public system also has but at a cost, and access to a wider range of services, private health insurance is likely to prove increasingly attractive to Australians. The more widespread use of private health insurance in the other countries also depends on the interplay of factors, many of which are similar to those already mentioned for Australia. Economic forces in particular are likely to be significant overriding factors in what eventually happens in many countries. In other words, these countries, virtually all burdened by escalating healthcare costs, would have to rethink their health financing models. In a paper titled, Limits of the market, constraints of the state: the public good and the NHS written for the Social Market Foundation, and published in February 2005 the UK Health Secretary John Reid argued for the need of a more consumer-oriented approach to healthcare delivery in order to secure the public's continuing support for state-funded health care. He contended that an increasingly educated and affluent society demanded greater choice and expected more from the NHS than the one size fits all model of yore. He asserted that only the affluent few had options in the health system in the past, but that the new approach, which he said would harness the best from the traditional public funding approach and the free market approach, would correct. The Health Secretary noted that patients would continue to choose NHS hospitals for most acute care, but government would use the independent sector much more to facilitate capacity expansion, and stimulate quality improvements, while protecting the founding principles of the NHS of equal access to health care provided free at the point of need. With the recent Supreme Court decision in Canada granting a Québécois legal backing to seek private healthcare, there are indications of more widespread use of private health insurance in the country as well, despite stiff opposition by some to what they consider violations of the fundamental values of Medicare as embodied in the Canada Health Act. Alberta, for example, seems to be heading for a confrontation over health care with Stephen Harper's new Conservative government with reports indicating that the province would soon allow queue jumping by patients willing to pay cash for treatments, the Prime Minister-elect insisting that the changes be made within the Canada Health Act. Two of the Act's provisions specifically discourage direct payments by patients via user charges or extra-billing, for services covered by Medicare, breach of which could attract heavy Federal financial penalties. On January 31, 2006, the Alberta cabinet received a nine-point health reform plan that would allow doctors to practice in both private and public systems, charging some patients directly and billing Medicare for others, although it is not clear if the cabinet approved the plan. However, the province's Health Minister, Iris Evans, said that she would discuss the plan and other aspects of Alberta's "Third Way" healthcare delivery proposals extensively with her Federal counterpart, on the latter's appointment. Incidentally, many Albertans protested in 1998 when Premier Ralph Klein's Tory government introduced Bill 11, which made for the increases in private clinics and might now have to go because it also prohibits queue jumping, although the Minister believes Albertans are now ready for new approaches to healthcare delivery, and looks forward to litheness on Ottawa's part. Besides the Supreme Court decision, Canada, like other countries, also recognizes the need to focus on population health and on the prevention of diseases and promotion of healthy living as ways by which it could reduce its increasing healthcare costs. The country is therefore investing substantially in healthcare ICT as previously noted, a move that would not only provide the necessary infrastructure to enable the achievement of the goals of population health, but also would help reduce healthcare costs by fostering cost-effective service delivery. South of Canada s border, in the US, there has also been significant changes in government s healthcare strategies. In his State of the Union speech delivered on January 31, 2006, President Bush gave health noticeable attention. Many of the president s proposals would have serious import for the health insurance industry. Consider the proposed expansion of the tax-free health savings accounts for example, which aims to increase consumer control over health expenses, as by the way does another of his proposals, that of expanding tax breaks for out-of-pocket health care costs. Expectedly, there have been divisions on the effects of these proposals. Some for instance think that expanding health savings accounts favors the older, affluent people, who could set aside more pre-tax dollars to save for current health expenses and medical expenses when they retire, unlike low and middle-income people with less disposable income whether pre-tax or not, to reserve for future healthcare payments, as those that oppose the plan note. Supporters of the plan also acknowledge that it might also work for younger persons who hardly incur health bills and might prefer to pay lower premiums in a high-deductible insurance plan. With regard expanding tax deductions for consumer healthcare expenses, many would argue that it would make tax code fairer to working poor and uninsured, who in the main pay for their healthcare out of pocket, but did not enjoy many of the tax benefits of employer-provided health plans. However, some would likely warn against the prospects of its abuse considering the difficulty in tracking vaguely defined healthcare expenses eligible for deductions, a situation that would result in lost tax revenues, the last thing a country with already high budget deficits needs. The President also mentioned the Medical Liability Reform Act as a means of reducing the spate of medical malpractice suits in the country that is not just inhibiting doctors in terms of the nature and scope of their practice, but is also making some patients apprehensive of receiving appropriate healthcare, the result of both, falling healthcare quality, but soaring costs. This proposal would likely prevent what some term "defensive medicine" whereby doctors order unnecessary lab tests to reduce the chances of law suits slammed against them, although some argue that the proposal would encourage negligence, doctors knowing there is a cap on liability. In any case, why should a negligent doctor expect not answer for it, the argument might further go.

There is little doubt that these proposals, if implemented, would have direct effects on the health insurance industry in the US. Significantly also in the President s speech for the industry, are his focus on technology, call for a bipartisan commission to examine the impact of baby boom retirement on Social Security, Medicare and Medicaid and recommend reforms, and his assertion that any country that covets isolationism would wither away. The health landscape of the US is changing fast, due among other reasons, to the increasing need for resources to accommodate the healthcare requirements of its aging population, a problem, common to virtually all developed countries. It is indisputable that chronic diseases are common in old age, that in general, it costs more to treat these conditions than non-chronic diseases, and that the costs are increasing for a variety of reasons including high hospitalization rates and the costs of prescription drugs. It is also increasingly clear that no country could afford to ignore global health issues, for example, HIV/ AIDS and avian flu, in an age when inter-continental flights only take a couple of hours. Finally, evidence already abounds of the value, tangible and intangible of healthcare ICT in the delivery of cost-effective and qualitative health services, and in preventing national, and cross-boundary disease transmission. Therefore, the link that binds the President s proposals together in many respects is healthcare ICT. It could dramatically reduce the costs of healthcare provision by helping to prevent diseases occurring in the first place, or via secondary prevention, ensure their prompt diagnosis and treatment, and tertiary prevention, minimize the burden in human and material terms, of their long-term sequelae. Healthcare ICT could facilitate the ambulatory and domiciliary management of chronic diseases, which would be certainly more empowering, and would enhance the quality of life of affected individuals treated in the company of their loved ones. This would reduce hospitalization rates and substantially reduce overall healthcare costs, without compromising service quality. Healthcare ICT would also facilitate the sort of international collaboration in both research and services required to combat imminent pandemics and other health issues that could affect people in all parts of the world, in the short or long term. This principle the world agrees on and as the pronunciations of world business, political, and opinion leaders who recently met at the World Economic Forum (WEF) in Davos, Switzerland, showed, isolationism runs counter to not just the achievement of global collaboration, but actually to the overall interests of any country.

Take the issue of hydrocarbon emissions for example. Researches have shown that the future of the world is at stake if it ignored the damages of these emissions to our climate, and by extension other key aspects of our lives. There is recent concern for example that the Greenland ice caps might be melting faster than we might ever have imagined, and which essentially fast-forwarded when rising sea levels would start to eat away coastlines around the world, even submerging some island states. Would it therefore not make sense in addition to tweaking market forces to also examine technological approaches, some of which, for example, subterranean siphoning of the gases have proven successful, to reducing the emissions of carbon dioxide and other hydrocarbons, including as the President proposed, exploring clean-energy options, including solar, wind and nuclear power? Would such efforts not also positively influence the health, of individuals and of society? What would the insurance industry benefit from a largely healthy populace? Would more people not be at work, offering services in their different jobs that would, on the aggregate foster sustainable economic prosperity? Would this not make even more resources available to fund health and social services and other services that we have come to take for granted in our age? In fact, would a healthy populace not create the enabling environment for the sort of creative intellectual endeavors that could result in the innovative discoveries that our planet needs to survive, discoveries that could help solve problems that threaten its very survival such as global warming? Would international cooperation on such projects not make it even likelier and quicker for solving many of the health problems facing humanity today? Some would argue that technology alone is not the answer to our problems. This is true. However, so is there not any other singular solution to these problems, the emphasis on population health mentioned perhaps one example of how technology could be the rallying focus of effective solutions to the variety of problems confronting modern humankind. No one could deny the fact that humans are the chief polluters of our world. We "scavenge" for survival in the process scorch the forests, hunt animals sometimes to extinction, and wreck havoc on nature, and now we must pay back, some would argue, but how? Reduce human population, and there would be less polluters, some would contend, an excellent point save we must then seek ways to achieve this goal. The goals of population health, which simply put is keeping everyone healthy, some would say runs counter to limiting the population. Yes, but only if one did not consider the significant role healthcare ICT could play in family planning, and in birth control, and is it not working in some countries, where the campaigns started with just the radio? Would most people not really appreciate the dangers for example to physical and psychological health of multiple pregnancies? Yet, no one would likely advocate for depleting the world of humankind. The issue no doubt involves striking the right balance in numbers, and includes creating the enabling environment for population redistribution so that we all do not cramp up in mega-cities with virtually no one living in the country. Furthermore, do we really have to ravage our environment? Could technology not help solve our seemingly insatiable survival needs? Does this ring true with President s Bush mention of nanotechnology in his recent State of the Union address? Why would we need to destroy the forests when we can essentially create wood with progress in nanotechnology perhaps a few years down the road? This is not at far-fetched. Nanotechnology predicates on the idea of building from the bottom up, from subatomic particles to tangible substances. In other words, the so-called human overpopulation issue warrants detailed analysis rather proffering one-track solutions to the problem. When in late 1959, Richard Feynman, who later won the Nobel prize in Physics, argued that the laws of physics need not limit our ability to manipulate individual atoms and molecules, his vision for constructing materials from the bottom, up, rather than the other way round, seemed far-fetched, but not anymore. A few decades from now, machines would be so small thousands of them would fit into an area the size of a period. Consumer goods would be manufactured from atoms and molecules, made possible by nanotechnology, which embraces many areas of research on incredibly small objects, measured in nanometers, one nanometer (nm) being a billionth of a meter, or a millionth of a millimeter. Nanotechnology aims to manipulate atoms individually and place them in a pattern to produce a desired structure, for example, using nanogears, about a nanometer wide, to construct a matter compiler, which would arrange atoms and construct a macro-scale structure. Progress in nanotechnology has been persistent since researchers at IBM showed, in 1990, that it was possible to manipulate individual atoms by positioning 35 xenon atoms on the surface of a nickel crystal. Nanomachines, termed assemblers, programmable to manipulate atoms and molecules and to construct products automatically exist. Nanomachines would be able to replicate anything eventually, from wood, to fabric, to water, even food. The effect of nanotechnology on the healthcare industry would be enormous, with engineers able to construct sophisticated nanorobots that could navigate the human body, transport molecules, manipulate objects, and communicate with doctors via miniature sensors, motors, manipulators, power generators and quantum computers. Nanorobots and smart drugs programmed to diagnose diseases and to attack and reconstruct the molecular structure of cancer cells and viruses, rendering them harmless, leaving healthy cells intact would feature in future pharmacopeia. Rather than use viruses stripped of their indigenous genes for gene-therapy trials, as is current practice, to carry therapeutic DNA into a target cell, starburst dendrimers, a class of synthetic molecules able to sneak into diseased cells without triggering an immune reaction as viruses often do would do the job instead. Cancer treatment may seem to be the main target of nanomedicine however; it would also be valuable in other areas for example, coordinating the activities of osteoblasts and osteoclasts, thus preventing osteoporosis. Nanorobots prescribed as a drink might also be able to slow or reverse aging. Nanorobots programmed to perform delicate, nanoscale potentially scar-free, surgeries might also be able to rearrange atoms to give someone an entirely new face. Artificial red blood cells would be able to provide metabolic support in case of compromised circulation by improving the levels of available oxygen despite reduced blood. Nanotechnology would positively affect the environment, reducing our dependence on non-renewable resources such as coal, by being able to construct them. Airborne nanorobots might in fact be able to rebuild the thinning ozone layer, and clean up oil spills. Would we have to ravage our environment if we invested significantly on research in nanotechnology and other promising technologies? There could be no gainsaying the importance of healthcare ICT and of technology in general in contemporary health services delivery. The health insurance industry could also not deny the tie between its survival and that of the health industry. If healthcare ICT could as the discussion thus far posits help the health industry survive by reducing healthcare costs while ensuring the delivery of qualitative health services, would it be irrational to expect the health insurance industry to tune-in to this new reality, and what would be the likely consequences if it did not? Is it also unreasonable to expect a paradigm shift in the health insurance in consonance with the far-reaching changes that now seem characteristic of the contemporary health industry? Certainly not, some would say, after all, it is a " health " insurance industry, and if the health industry ceased to exist, all other industries tied to it would soon be moribund. This is a truism. However, the reality is more complex. Suffice to say that it is difficult to see how the health insurance industry could ignore the increasing tendency of the health industry toward the free market and not in fact need a new paradigm to survive in a decidedly and increasingly hyper-competitive business milieu.

References

1. Available at: http://www.chron.com/cs/CDA/printstory.mpl/nation/3622861 Accessed on January 31, 2006

2. Available at: http://www.sweden.gov.se/content/1/c6/05/05/67/e93ce32b.pdf Accessed on January 31, 2006

3. Available at: http://www.canada.com/topics/news/national/story.html?id=5783cb2b-2f12-4a7a-96ab-f7697aa334f1&k=9154 Accessed on February 01, 2006

Conclusions

Progress in technology is helping the health industry achieve its goals of reducing health costs while simultaneously providing qualitative healthcare. One of the most critical benefits of healthcare ICT deployment is in facilitating real time access to vital patient data and information at the point of care (POC). Wireless technology for example is increasingly important in this regard, which faster connections and wider broadband has made possible in recent times. Public expectations of healthcare services for example continue to be high. Technologies such as mobile and wireless are helping meet some of these expectations. Patients and their relatives for example can now watch television, listen to the radio and surf the Internet without having to leaving the emergency room (ER), and with regard to the patient, his or her ER bed, although such services fall under the non-clinical services that some recommend should attract user fees even in publicly funded systems. ER departments, for example that of the new $3.1-million 10,000-square-foot emergency care department Florida's Sun Coast Hospital, phase I of which it opened on January 17, 2006, now offer a variety of wireless-based valued-added services to their clients. The Hospital s Patientline, a computer/ television terminal that allows patients to check e-mail, use the phone, and to watch television, typifies the meaning of consumer-driven healthcare, which increasingly more healthcare stakeholders now embrace. When operational in full, the facility would offer even more technology-enabled services. Physicians would be able to review lab work results and other patient information on the computer screen, and patients able to get on the Internet via wireless network connections in the waiting room while waiting to see the doctor. Physicians could use a computer terminal in each patient room to access patient medical records and view lab results or do so via their mobile devices; emergency room staff would be able to use the wireless network to sign in patients more proficiently and speed up patients access to doctors. With the new wireless technologies, ER staffers would be able to register patients at their bedsides, thereby reducing time spent waiting for that purpose in the waiting room. Generally, ER staffers take up to an hour to fill out paperwork for every hour of care. These new technologies would result in better time management: less time spent filling out

145

forms, fewer patient record loss, and more effective service provision. Suncoast's paperless environment would also allow physicians to access digital X-rays from several workstations instead of having to look at the actual X-ray films. Its new ER would also have a new glass-enclosed waiting room where it would offer wireless technology to patients and their caretakers, enabling them to access the Internet on their personal digital assistants (PDAs) or notebooks, giving them something to do other than watch TV. What are the technologies behind these valuable functionalities? Intel officially launched its first WiMAX chipset, the Intel PRO/ Wireless 5116 chip, termed Rosedale, on April 18, 2005. WiMAX means Worldwide Interoperability for Microwave Access. This people-friendly moniker for the IEEE 802.16 standard is the certification name, the standard best suited for delivering non-line-of-sight (NLOS) wireless broadband access to both fixed and nomadic users. Did the chip signal a new epoch of wireless broadband access? Some would say, may be not, as the 802.16-2004 standard or WiMAX received approval in 2004 but the equipment has to wait for interoperability testing. Furthermore, the mobile edition of the standard (802.16e) needs to wait even longer. Estimated commencement of certification for mobile WiMAX is mid-2006, when the certification labs open, with the first certified products available in the first quarter of 2007. Prior to then, WiMAX would have to vie with fixed broadband such as DSL, T1 and cable, with mobile devices such as notebooks and PDAs, also having to wait to be WiMAX-enabled. In other words, two important functionalities of WiMAX technologies for healthcare delivery portability, and mobility access, would have to wait, a key point that insurers and interested stakeholders need to know in developing their healthcare ICT strategy. Indeed, on 19 January 2006, the WiMAX Forum, an industry-led, non-profit corporation formed to promote and certify compatibility and interoperability of broadband wireless products, announced the first fixed wireless broadband network products to achieve the designation of WiMAX Forum Certified. Revealed at the WCA Technical and Business Symposium in San Jose, the first companies and products to complete certification and interoperability testing, include Aperto Networks PacketMAX 5000 base station, Redline Communications RedMAX AN-100U base station, SEQUANS Communications SQN2010 SoC base station solution, and Wavesat's miniMAX customer premise equipment (CPE) solution. The development of the products followed the WiMAX Forumdefined certification profile for 3.5 GHz systems, based on the IEEE 802.16-2004 and ETSI HiperMAN standards, each hardware system required to pass stringent and extensive test procedures, including protocol conformance, radio conformance and interoperability testing.

WiMAX, designed for metropolitan area networks (MAN) has not replaced but complemented Wi-Fi, which stands for wireless fidelity, actually designed for local area networks (LAN) by extending its reach and providing a "Wi-Fi like" user experience but wider coverage. Between 2006-2008, both 802.16 (WiMAX) and 802.11(Wi-Fi) will be available in end user devices from laptops to PDAs, delivering wireless connectivity directly to the end user, stationary or mobile, when the health industry would be able to reap full benefits from these technologies. The new generation of 3G such as HSDPA and 1xEV-DO Rev A, are offering even more functionalities. Evolution Data Optimized (EV-DO) is a secure technology designed for service providers rather than the home and corporate environment. Code Division Multiple Access (CDMA)-based, it is a third-generation (3G) broadband wireless packet data technology, optimized for high-speed mobile data applications. EV-DO is already providing fully mobile wireless broadband services, also has speed advantage, and has wider coverage and superior network economics than Wi-Fi or WiMAX. Eavesdropping is also unknown with CDMA-based voice systems, unlike seen with several other wireless voice technologies, and EV-DO standard offers several levels of access control or authentication. Nonetheless, Wi-Fi clouds are increasingly gaining currency in many cities, although there are questions regarding the efficiency of this technology. Meanwhile the Bluetooth Special Interest Group and Ultrawideband developers have collaborated to resolve the incompatibility of their wireless networking technologies. Some of these incompatible networking technologies include Zigbee, Wi-Fi, Ultrawideband, Bluetooth, and Near Field Communications. By making these technologies compatible, developers and end user alike would be able to enjoy the high transfer rates of the Ultrawideband technology on a variety of devices that use Bluetooth such as mobile phones and other handheld devices, which are becoming more commonly sued in the health industry. This was a major boost in transfer speed as Ultrawideband speeds range between 100 megabits and 200 megabits over a range of 10- to 20-feet. The decision to make these technologies compatible would facilitate the evolution of digital media, among other benefits, and augurs well for profitability as some SIG members such as Motorola and Intel, also have major stakes in Ultrawideband specifications. Bluetooth consumes little power hence better suits mobile phones whereas Wi-Fi has a broader spectrum but needs more battery power. Faster transfer speeds make it easier for end users to send and receive data with any of these devices. While experts are already predicting the development of products capable of using the combined technologies, progress continues apace with new technologies, for example, impulse-radio ultra-wideband (IR-UWB), which may result in self-organizing wireless personal area networks, emerging. According to researchers working under the Information Society Technologies (IST), project Ultra-wideband Concepts for Ad-hoc Networks (UCAN,) who recently developed a complete UWB system, UWB is useful for communication, ranging, and localization, works up to 10 meters, with ranging accuracy up to 15 centimeters in line of sight. Impulse-radio UWB is superior to other short-range wireless technologies, which, for example, Bluetooth, utilizes more power and cannot do localization. Radio frequency identification (RFID) has a very short range, most applications utilizing uniquely the passive tags, without batteries. Because impulse-radio UWB spreads energy over the bandwidth at low peak power, it would not conflict with other short-range technologies. UWB, based on Direct Sequence Spread-Spectrum (DSSS) modulation, promoted mainly by Freescale focuses on two sorts of application in the short-range IEEE 802.15 technologies: low-range, high-throughput (IEEE 802.15.3a) and low power, low-complexity/ sensor networks (the 802.15.4a version). Health insurers need to appreciate the effects emerging technologies would have on their operations, including on billing for services provided by doctors and other healthcare professionals, via devices such as mobile phones and PDAs.

Technology is just one aspect of the multiplicity of factors impinging on the health industry that would directly or other affect the health insurance industry. Yet, it is one the underlines many of the new concepts that are changing the healthcare delivery landscape. In his 2006 State of the Union speech, the US President, George Bush reaffirmed his commitment to providing Americans with electronic health records (EHR). The President stated that government will make wider use of electronic medical records and other health information technology to help control costs and reduce dangerous medical errors". These objectives reflect two of the major concerns that the health industry, in collaboration with the health insurance industry must address, and healthcare ICT could indeed, help in achieving these goals. The President also stressed the need for the US to eschew isolationism, which suggests that the country is willing to operate in the global arena, including in the global health arena, collaborating with other countries in tackling problems common to all humankind that threaten its very existence, for example, an avian flu pandemic. In order to participate in the global health community, it has to take its own health seriously, which explain the President s proposals to invest more in healthcare ICT to meet the challenge of rising health costs, which by extension represents significant costs to business and industry as well. EHR is the bedrock of efforts to exploit the many benefits of healthcare ICT. Health insurance and other businesses have vested interested in supporting government efforts to implement nationwide electronic health information networks including EHR. These efforts do not just mean offering incentives to healthcare providers to implement healthcare ICT, including electronic medical records (EMR), but also promoting the acceptance of these technologies by the public, current efforts along which direction seem to be working. The public is not only increasingly embracing the idea of EHR; many are actually buying-in into the idea of online personal health records (PHR). Indeed, private organizations are emerging that provide Internet-based PHR services for individuals. The idea of PHR, despite concerns about privacy and confidentiality seems increasingly attractive as it provides individuals some measure of control over their personal health information, the information accessible only to the individuals and those that they authorized. MyMedicalRecords.com, one of such companies noted that healthcare experts agree that reductions in healthcare costs that would result if every American had an electronic patient health record would be almost US$1000 billion yearly. Furthermore, by the combination of benefits of such records within a more pervasive EHR systems also reducing medical errors, morbidities, and mortalities, premiums would fall, businesses would have a more productive workforce, and health insurance firms would become more profitable. Indeed, collaborative efforts on patient formation already exists, exemplified by the formation of regional health information networks in the US, for example, recently by a group of physician practices, a hospital, and insurer, which formed the Integrated Physician Network Avista, in the Boulder, Colorado, area. The group s leaders include Clinica Campesina Family Health Services, a federally qualified medical center; Colorado Access, an insurer serving the medically underserved; and 14 private physician practices with 19 locations. The Regional Health Information Organizations (RHIO) concentrates on improving care for the uninsured and those not enrolled in Medicare and Medicaid. Participating physicians, 108 in all, will be able to access the same electronic health records (EHR) software, integrated with the Medical Information Technologies information system of Avista Adventist Hospital. Indeed, the network also has just finished a laboratory interface with Quest Diagnostics. This is the emerging, technology-backed, healthcare milieu in the US. All the RHIOs in the country would link with the national health information network (NHIN), the development of prototypes for which, expected by the fall, 2006. RHIOs will have local flavors in terms of value-added service provision depending on the specific needs of the populations that they serve. However, the final objectives would be the same nationwide. RHIOs will support local stakeholders in some way, and as the NHIN prototypes take shape, may need to more or less modify their business models and market approaches so that they could participate well in the NHIN.

The Office of the National Coordinator for health information technology (ONC) in the US has four stated sequential goals as parts of its vision of the future of healthcare in the country, namely, informing clinicians, interconnecting them, personalizing care, and thus improving population health. These goals speak eloquently to the central role of healthcare ICT in the future of healthcare in the country. Indeed, as the ONC clearly states "Our fourth and final goal is the most challenging and far-reaching but also the most important-improving the health of the entire nation. This task cannot .contemplated without timely and accurate information. But with a concerted and unified effort at all levels of government and private endeavor, a strong foundation for population health can be attained. The ONC thus reaffirms the need not just for healthcare ICT in meeting the objectives of population health, and albeit, all other goals it has set to achieve, but that for collaboration among stakeholders. The ONC further states, " To accomplish this ultimate goal, the federal government has proposed three primary strategies: unifying public health surveillance systems; streamlining quality and health status monitoring; and accelerating the pace at which scientific discoveries in medicine are disseminated into medical practice." The emphasis of the ONC on research and medical progress underscores the point that stakeholders, including the health insurance industry cannot afford to ignore developments in medical research and practice. In particular, with regard to the health insurance industry, medical knowledge is changing so rapidly that an insurer that failed to keep abreast of this changing knowledge risks compromising its competitiveness, and indeed, its very survival. To buttress the point that collaboration is key to getting any national health information network off the ground, Florida, awarded over $1.5 Million for EHRs in a recent announcement by its Lt. Governor Toni Jennings and Agency for Health Care Administration (AHCA) Secretary Alan Levine, joined by representatives of the Tampa Bay Regional Health Information Organization. The announcement named the recipients of the Florida Health Information Network (FHIN) grants on January 6, 2006, the grants designed to facilitate the adoption and use of privacy-protected electronic health records in the State. In 2005, the Florida Legislature appropriated $1.5 million to fund the development of the FHIN, and in 2006, the State Governor Jeb Bush will request $5 million in recurring funding for additional grants to support broadening the scope of EHRs. Also in the US, the Michigan Governor Jennifer M. Granholm, launched a Statewide Health Information Network, outlined in a three-step plan to bring healthcare delivery into the 21st century during her January 25 State of the State Address, chief among which is the use of technology, to improve the health system. According to the Governor, " In the future, you will be able to give your pharmacist, your doctor, or the emergency room immediate access to your information, but you will control who sees it and what it is used for. Think about it, never having to remember the name of the medicines you have been prescribed. Never having to fill out another form detailing your medical history, your allergies, and the last time your 10-year-old got a tetanus shot. Gov. Granholm also plans to introduce a new insurance product called the Michigan First Health Care Plan and public-private partnerships to promote a culture of physical activity, prevention, and wellness in the state. Do these plans not clearly indicate the focus of healthcare in the future? The private sector is also actively involved in promoting healthcare ICT. The Robert Wood Johnson Foundation (RWJF) in the US recently funded 21 grants, up to $100,000 each, to state and local health departments and public health institutes for 12-month projects, named InformationLinks, designed to quicken ICT use by state and local public health agencies.

While many governments recognize the need to invest in healthcare ICT, financial constraints combined with the sometimes-substantial financial outlay some of these technologies demand threatens their widespread adoption. A report published in the Daily Mail on February 3, 2006 for example noted that the extra money pumped into the NHS in England in the next year would go into pay rises and increased drugs costs, according to an analysis by The King's Fund health think-tank. The think-tank analyzed data from the Department of Health. Specifically, it suggested that almost 40% of the £4.5 billion cash increase for hospital and community health services for 2006/07 would go into funding staff pay rises, an additional 32% of the extra money, into higher prices and increases in costs linked to recommendations by the National Institute for Health and Clinical Excellence (NICE), clinical negligence and capital costs. This means only 28% or about £1.26 billion left for other developments for example reducing waiting times and other Government priorities. Indeed, the briefing paper titled, "Where's the money going?" also noted that projected NHS deficit for the end of this financial year would be the largest since the Labor government came to power, the six-month projection, more than £500 million for 2005/06, expect to fall significantly by the end of the financial year. The Government has deployed its "turnaround teams" into 18 NHS trusts to assist in solving their financial problems, as John Appleby, King's Fund chief economist, noted, the new data clearly is an indication of the financial pressure the NHS currently faces. This situation is not peculiar to the NHS, and paradoxically, is one that healthcare ICT could help turn around. By helping to rationalize drug prescribing, reducing medical errors, enabling patients and doctors to discuss options including cost considerations, and indeed, by helping prevent illness in the first place, and reducing morbidities, healthcare ICT could significantly reduce drugs costs. It would be prudent therefore, to invest rather than not in order to turn the NHS financial difficulties around for example. Indeed, there should be increasing focus on various aspects of the applications of ICT in healthcare delivery, as for example the plan of the US federal advisory body to commence work on projects that range from strengthening the U.S. healthcare system's public health event monitoring network to enabling consumers to have access to personal health records (PHR.). The American Health Information Community (AHIC) concluded at its meeting on January 31, 2006 in Washington, D.C., will collate recommendations in a year including that of a biosurveillance work group that would enable within a year, sending ambulatory and emergency department data in a standardized, de-identified format to public health agencies within 24 hours. AHIC also expects recommendations from a chronic care work group that will explore how widespread use of secure messaging could help clinicians and patients communicate. It also expects suggestions from a consumer empowerment work-group on how to make a pre-populated, secure electronic registration summary available to certain populations, and on ways to make a medication history linked to the registration summary widely available within a year. AHIC also looks forward to ideas from an EHR work group on how to make standardized, current, and historical lab data available for clinical care. These conclusions reiterate the importance of collaboration of a wide variety of government and private organizations and individuals in seeking and implementing solutions to healthcare problems, including assuring the quality of healthcare delivery, and reducing soaring health costs, and in promoting healthcare ICT diffusion. There is no doubt that the recommendations of the various work groups, which also highlight the role newer technologies would play in health services delivery, would help in achieving these objectives. There is no disputing the fact many see the human factor increasingly as just as important as technological progress and capital accumulation, and indeed, other factors, in economic development. This explains the increasing appreciation of the concept of population health, which many governments are making a priority and would become even more relevant in years ahead, which is inevitable if health is no longer simply the absence of disease and if we conceptualized overpopulation in realistic terms. In particular, we need not panic about medical progress reducing mortality and leaving fertility intact, as Winslow[1] advised back in 1951 in his 'Interrelationships of poverty and disease', in a World Health Organization (WHO) monograph that year. Debate over whether we should preserve health for those prior to or in the productive life stages, or put differently whether we should concern ourselves with present or future generations linger on, exemplified by arguments over age-weighted Disability-

/Quality-Adjusted Life-year (DALY/ QUALY) measurements. However, the acute realization of the economic devastation of HIV/ AIDS[2] and Sen s[3] works on human capabilities have brought the idea of disease/ death prevention as drivers of population efficiency , and from which human capital theory evolved in the 1960s squarely back to the fore. Far from conceptualizing human beings as means of production or simply in material terms, current concepts of sustainable development embrace the ideas of human aspirations, and development and what Winslow termed "man-with-nature", which provide the intellectual cobblestone of the quest to redress inequity and inequality in all aspects of our lives, including in healthcare delivery. The logical extension of this quest is the concept of population health, and indeed, a collaborative national, and international approach to health exemplified by the Sector-Wide Approach (SWAP), an agreement by developed countries, the International Monetary Fund (IMF), and the World Bank, and the recent financial commitment of several countries to a common global war against the avian flu menace. There is no doubt that investing in health could negate poverty in any society, and that healthcare ICT could help both developed and developing countries achieve this goal, albeit, with healthcare ICT strategies tailored to meet specific needs of each country, and within the context of its established institutions and infrastructure.

Regardless of whether a country's health system is insurance or tax-financed, the ultimate goal should be for all its peoples to receive qualitative healthcare rooted in preventive health principles. In any case, the difference between them mostly pertains to ownership and operations of hospitals and other healthcare institutions, with private (companies, trusts, and organizations) ownership in insurance-financed healthcare systems, publicly owned in countries with tax financing, although there is some degree of private sector in ownership and operation of these institutions in some of these countries. The differences with regard financing are even less in reality, with insurance contributions based on income, and deducted when income taxes are. Private insurance also have equalization principles, although many query their effectiveness in many countries, for example the US, which explains why some welcome many of the proposals in President Bush's 2006 State of the Union Speech. For example, the idea of coupling bare-bones, high-deductible insurance policy with an account into which people can

154

deposit money tax-free, which they could later use for medical expenses, giving individuals a greater financial stake in obtaining reasonably priced care, which by increasing competition, would force prices down, making healthcare more affordable, and many more individuals thus able to receive it. Indeed, proponents would argue, this would ultimately contribute to reducing the country's overall health costs. The president's plans would increase the annual amounts that people can contribute tax-free to their health savings accounts from the current maximums of $2,700 for individuals and $5,450 for families to $5,250 and $10,500, respectively, which proponents say would enable individuals to pay all of their out-of-pocket medical expenses tax-free. Some contend the accuracy of the estimates, and in particular, the idea of allowing payment for the premiums for the bare bones insurance policies with the tax-free funds, which they argue would deplete the latter leaving little if anything left, especially for poor families, to out-of-pocket medical expenses. A counter-argument would be why insurance premiums and indeed, out-of-pocket expenses, should be high in the first place. Just as shopping around for cost-effective treatment would force prices down, premiums are also subject to market forces. In fact, it is not always in the interest of insurance firms for premiums to be high, as they could still operate profitably with most clients being healthy, in which case, premiums would drop, or the insurer would soon be out of business. Here again, the value of disease prevention becomes clear, as is the role healthcare ICT could play in achieving it as rectifying information asymmetry, public health education, disease surveillance, and health promotion, among other public health measures predicate on the effective use of ICT. Insurers and healthcare providers have a major role to play in making the President's plans work, by making pricing and chargemasters, respectively available to the public, a measure that also implementing the appropriate healthcare ICT would facilitate. The president has proposed over the years the low-income tax credit, essentially that persons making up to $15,000 and families, up to $25,000 would be eligible for $1,000 and $3,000 credits, respectively, to assist in funding traditional comprehensive insurance, but in the new proposal, low-income families would only be eligible for the credit if they buy bare-bones policies. This new twist some would regard as inherently unfair to low-income earners but others would see as an attempt at equitable healthcare delivery by preventing abuse and overuse of tax credits, which could further escalate healthcare spending. Another proposed measure that is brewing controversy is preempting state regulation of insurance policies used to qualify for some health savings accounts, which the Federal government hopes would also help reduce the cost of policies by protecting them from costly state mandates. Although some believe the breaches federalism principles, some would argue it is the key to the success of the other proposals. Proponents would likely cite the Bush's administration recent extension of 60 days to the previous 30, for health insurers to provide beneficiaries of the Medicare prescription-drug plan benefits started on January 01, 2006, emergency supply of any drugs they were taking before the Medicare prescription drug benefit started as evidence that it is not necessarily on the insurers side. The Department of Health and Human Services (HHS) noted that 60-day extension to the 30-day transitional coverage, required under the 2003 Medicare law, would allow beneficiaries more time to consider switching to less costly alternatives to their current medications, which as previously mentioned might eventually reduce overall health costs. With the observation of the HHS Secretary Mike Leavitt, that competition among private plans has led to lower costs under the new benefit, and that the Federal government will spend about 20% less per beneficiary in 2006 than previously estimated, and over the next five years, payments likely will be at least 10% lower than first estimated. Leavitt said that projected enrollment in the benefit has not changed significantly, the plan seems to be yielding expected results. This is not to say that everything has been smooth sailing since January 01, 2006, as the Secretary in fact admitted initial difficulties implementing the plan, most observers have noted were administrative in nature, and due in the main to flawed ICT planning. This again underscores the central role that ICT plays in contemporary health insurance, and need for a well thought-out healthcare ICT strategy in order to achieve the objectives of the new health paradigm. Furthermore, insurers also have to wait out the outcomes of the lawsuits some states plan to file against the Federal government for alleged over-billing for the cost of prescription drugs for dual eligibles. At least 15 governors claim that this would result in their states spending more under the Medicare drug benefit through fiscal year 2006-2007 than they would have spent if they had continued offering prescription drug coverage to dual eligibles through Medicaid. California, for example, such extra costs to be $161 million by mid-2007, although the Federal government insists states would actually save money and that their calculations of losses overlooked the assistance that the federal government is providing for the costs of prescription drugs for state employees. Clearly, the future of health insurance would depend on a combination of factors least of which is government policy, reforms, and regulation. Healthcare costs would underpin many of these reforms and regulations, and healthcare ICT would play a leading role since it has the potential to reduce costs even if it takes some time for this to show. Also in the US, Medicare officials on February 02, 2006[4] said that the new prescription-drug benefit would cost taxpayers less than originally estimated, even, as mentioned earlier, some states are taking the Federal government to court over the program's costs, specifically for, as they claim, having to reimburse Medicare for more than they saved. States have to reimburse the Federal Medicare because the federal program provides drugs to some state Medicaid patients. Medicare officials indicated that cost estimates fell substantially in less than a month after the drug plan took off, the government's estimated 10-year cost dropping from $737 billion projected in 2005 to $678 billion, although still more than the initial $400 billion cost estimate. Premiums for persons that signed up for the program, an average of $25 a month, compared with $37 a month projected in July 2005, which officials credited to stronger-than-expected competition, itself due to lower drug costs. Could these projections change over the years, for worse for example, and could healthcare ICT not further reduce medication costs, hence premium costs, while in fact also improving the quality of healthcare delivery and ensure the changes are positive down the road? Would it still be necessary for the States threatening to sue the Federal government to actualize their plan considering that they would not have to reimburse the federal government as much for drugs used by the elderly and disabled already covered by Medicaid? These multfactorial influences are changing health insurance in other countries too. In Germany for example, hospitals customarily received their payments from social insurance funds based to the number of hospital days, which along hospital bed per population ration is much higher than for most other countries. In recent times, the health system in Germany is also under severe strain, due to rapidly increasing health costs, which the country is also seeking ways to reduce relying substantially on healthcare ICT. There is likely to influence competition among health insurers, which would have to depend paradoxically on healthcare ICT to enhance their value propositions in order to remain afloat. Competition is another key factor at play in healthcare delivery these days, even in countries with publicly funded health systems. This tendency among others predicates on research studies comparing the UK NHS with Kaiser Health system in the US, which revealed consistently after adjusting for age distribution, the two healthcare systems provided similar health services at the same cost, but that the latter provided faster access to primary, hospital, and specialist care. Some contend that these findings support the need for competition and a free-market health system. While Kaiser Doctors cannot operate private practice, the organization competes in the private insurance-based US health system, and seems to be quite successful at doing so. Indeed, some studies showed that healthcare cost at Kaiser Permanente was less than half the average cost in the US. Success at Kaiser, which bears similarities with the UK publicly funded system, many claim results from their integration of finance and service provision, which of course, the implementation of the appropriate healthcare ICT underlie, a clear example of how such technologies could help reduce healthcare costs. Companies and other employers would likely play increasing roles in the health system, their decisions, likely to influence the health insurance industry substantially, as did those of Eastman Kodak and Xerox in Rochester, NY, in the 1990s. Some would argue that, the experiment, whereby the city at the companies behest developed a healthcare system that essentially eschewed competition and embraced collaboration between insurers, failed. Others would hail the system s high-quality low cost healthcare, less than a third of the country s average, and that over 95% of the people had health insurance cover in the early 19990s. However, there were already threats to the systems. The role that some claim the emergent Medical Diagnosis-Related Group (DRG) system in the 1980s in the eventual demise of the experiment is arguable, but the lesson seems clear, that is, competition is essentially a survival game, the arena where costs issues ultimately play out. Interest in the application of ICT in healthcare delivery continues in different parts of the world. On February 03, 2006, in Brussels, European Health and Consumer Protection Commissioner Markos Kyprianou launched the "European Health Information Platform" or "Health in Europe" project. This health information system, co-financed with ᶜ1.4 million from the EU Public Health Program, and managed by the European Broadcasting Union (EBU), is a multimedia initiative aimed at creating a network of public broadcasters and other media in different countries in Europe. It also aims to foster the exchange of reports; including television documentaries, radio broadcasts, and press and internet articles on health issues, a key step toward rectifying the asymmetry of health information that is still rife, even in Europe. According to the Commissioner, "This partnership of TV and radio networks across Europe through the European Broadcasting Union will help keep citizens, and in particular patients and health professionals, informed on public health issues with a European dimension." The basis of Health in Health in Europe is an ongoing exchange of reports on health and medicine that TV broadcasters produce for their theme magazines, these reports, given rights-free to participating agencies, the times regularly reviewed. T V still being the medium of choice to reach the largest possible audiences in Europe explains its prominence but the Internet will also play a major role in the project. As individuals learn more about their health and about diseases and how to prevent them, they would likely be more open to embracing healthcare ICT, including being more willing to use personal health records and have their health information in electronic health records systems. Concerns about privacy in the past have hampered progress with not only ICT diffusion but also regarding exploiting the benefits of technologies to the fullest. The Journal of Biomedical Informatics in September last year, for example reported such concerns were hindering efforts to spot disease clusters and monitor the health effects of environmental pollution, despite that data available to research groups investigating cancer clusters, for example is often restricted, altered or aggregated to ensure the privacy of individual patients. These measures, however, make it difficult if not impossible to conduct accurate geographical analyses of public health concerns, and may even lead to the use of misleading information in healthcare decisions. There is no doubt that this does not convince with the goals of population health. However, technological innovation could help solve this problem, although it is important to continue also to pursue confidence-building measures such as that rectifying current and preventing further information asymmetry could accomplish. New technology that uses software "agents" to explore data should provide healthcare professionals with more accurate and meaningful information yet protecting patients identities, software programs able to set an explicit task, but then allowed the freedom to set goals and conduct operations required to actualize them, including being responsive to the environment and interacting and cooperating with other agents. Collaborating bodies could provide raw data for research in secure virtual milieu in which the gents could operate. These technologies would likely revolutionize public health research and programs, and help to identify the risk factors within our environment that we all face, and other health issues, in effect facilitating the achievement of the goals of population health. The achievement of which goals, being the most fundamental objective of the new healthcare zeitgeist, by extension becomes the imperative, that propels the actualization of the new health insurance paradigm.

Recent developments in Germany also typify the delicate interactions between technology, insurance, and health. The country has typically spent little on health healthcare ICT, just about 0.5% of its health expenditure, relative to other developed countries. However, this is changing, as the need for healthcare ICT continues to increase due to a combination of factors, namely, the shift in emphasis toward integrated healthcare ICT policy, which less than 20% of German hospitals currently embrace, the country's new reimbursement structures, and certain initiatives by government, among others. The country lagged behind other European countries in embracing integrated healthcare ICT partly because it hitherto lacked a coherent Federal eHealth focus, decentralization of healthcare administration resulting in wide variations and inconsistencies of healthcare ICT policies, strategies, and implementation, and increasingly tight health ICT budgets, among others. The change in emphasis would result in more investment in healthcare ICT aimed at integrating the hospital, and ambulatory care sectors of the German health system. The new country's new hospital billing system, based on diagnosis-related groups (DRGs) would also stimulate healthcare ICT investments and market growth. So would the healthcare reforms Acts promulgated in recently giving healthcare ICT priority status, and triggering Federal government plans to invest in a variety of healthcare ICT projects including e-prescriptions, electronic health records (EHR), personal health records (PHR), healthcare professional cards. The Health Ministry has recently released its master plan for "Information Technology Society Germany 2006," which emphasized that these projects would be at national, and not just at Länder levels, as in the past. The country also has new laws mandating digitalizing all patient information and procedure data going to the sickness funds for reimbursement. There are also new regulations regarding reimbursement for in-patient treatment post DRGs- introduction. Compliance with these regulations and laws require healthcare ICT investments many healthcare providers cannot afford to shun. In any case, many of these establishments are beginning to realize that that it is in their best interest to invest in healthcare ICT anyway because of increased awareness of its potential to streamline and improve their work processes, efficiencies, and productivity, cost-effectively. These developments are certainly going to make the healthcare ICT markets increasingly attractive to software and ICT vendors in the years ahead, certainly worth much more than the just over 1 billion Euro that it was three years ago, the estimated yearly growth for the clinical systems market, up to 20%, for the administrative systems markets, about 6%. Canada has a new Conservative government that is committed to upholding the Canada Health Act. This means that the government would be against any measures provincial and territorial governments take that run counter to the Act, and has indicated its willingness to uphold the Act in its response to Alberta s latest private healthcare moves. Uncertainty looms over the country's health system considering the recent Supreme Court s decision to allow private healthcare in Quebec, and this would no doubt affect the pace and intensity of healthcare ICT investment in the country. There has been a significant increase in this regard in recent times, driven in the main by primary care reforms, including a stronger emphasis on population health. Healthcare authorities in the country are also eager to reduce wait times in hospitals across the country, and to contain spiraling healthcare costs, both of which there is consensus that healthcare ICT could help achieve. Canada has a large land mass and its population though concentrated along its southern strip, is also widely dispersed geographically, and with the country short of healthcare professionals has had little choice than to rely on the healthcare ICT, specifically, telehealth, to facilitate healthcare delivery to its peoples living in remote areas. The country has a long history of telehealth deployment. It would likely continue to utilize this means extensively in healthcare delivery in the years ahead. It would also likely to invest even more in healthcare ICT, over its $1.5 billion between 1997 and 2003, in its pursuit of qualitative healthcare delivery. By investing more in healthcare ICT, it would also hope to reduce its massive health spending, projected in 2005 at $142 billion, about 10.4% of the country s GDP (10.1% in 2004), the highest ever, according to data the Canadian Institute for Health Information

(CIHI) released on December 07, 2005. Overall increase in health spending over 2004, 7.7%, and adjusted for inflation rate 5.5%. The Canada would witness a heightened interplay of the technology, health, and insurance trio, if private healthcare took off in earnest, particularly if the courts made similar rulings in other provinces as the Supreme Court did in Quebec. In this case, market forces would take over this tripartite situation with profound effects on each of its components and on the Canadian economy in general. Competition and collaboration would occur in various combinations among healthcare providers, healthcare ICT a major driver of these events. In other words, there would likely be proliferation of private healthcare providers, conventional and otherwise, all striving to outmaneuver their competition via technology-based value added services. It would then no longer be just going to one s GP and sitting, and just waiting. Some GPs might even have a playroom for their clients children complete with X-Box and other computer games. Clients might be able to surf the Internet while they wait to see their doctors. GPs might have an adjacent wellness center equipped fully with the latest gadgets and perhaps tailored for different ages and gender. Many GPs would have to merge to survive, particularly in the face of stiff competition from home and abroad. Venture capitalists would likely be all over the country, building sophisticated specialist clinics equipped with the latest healthcare technologies. Meantime, the public health systems would have to buck up or wither away. There would likely be a spate of closure of hospitals, no longer financially viable, as government efforts shift toward ambulatory and domiciliary care, which, in keeping with its population health goals would increasingly become its forte. Government would also step in, albeit cautiously to ensure the smooth operations of this new free-health market, and to protect the interests, in particular, of those of its peoples that would still depend exclusively on Medicare, and those that use the private health system. These developments would likely require revisiting the country s overall social and welfare services policies, as well as pension reforms, and reimbursement systems for doctors and other healthcare professionals. With regard to the latter, any large scale, private healthcare operations in the country would likely further tip the balance of the distribution of healthcare professionals, necessitating novel approaches to recruitment and retention policies for these personnel cadres. In short, any dramatic changes to the country s present healthcare system would result in changes in several aspects of its policy domains in equal measure. It would likely take some time for Canadians to acclimatize to these changes, which incidentally, would likely be in their favor in the long term, as competition would likely have an aggregate effect of reducing the costs of health insurance premiums, and their out-of-pocket healthcare expenses, while they would receive improved quality healthcare to the bargain. These positive effects, however, may not be immediately obvious, but would with time. As previously noted, no one knows if this scenario would materialize. What is less uncertain is that even without the change-provoking effects of market forces, and if the country ran only a publicly funded health system, healthcare ICT would trigger major changes in health service provision in the country. Canadians expect much from their health system, particularly one on which their governments at Federal/ provincial/ territorial levels are spending such a sizeable chunk of the country s resources. These expectations, increasingly sophisticated as they are, would continue to drive the quest for improvements in healthcare delivery, for example, wait times reduction. This would necessitate continued and indeed, increased healthcare ICT investments, having become clear that these technologies could help improve healthcare delivery while saving costs.

Private health insurance would continue to create controversy hotbeds in many countries, and its position would likely become increasingly tenuous within the trio, as changes in the other two, which are increasingly frequent and intense, would have far-reaching implications for the health insurance industry. Consider the seeming spread of the new UK "supersurgery" phenomenon to the US, with people seeking medical attention in their neighborhood grocery store these days, confident that they would save money by saving a trip to the ER, yet get expected results. According to press reports, many more stores, ranging for small-scale chains such as Bultez' local Hy-Vee to megamarkets such as Wal-Mart and Target, have begun trial runs with in-store medical clinics. Reports indicate that retailers are venturing outside their traditional domains into healthcare essentially to buoy foot traffic rather than an attempt to create a new revenue stream, but these forays seems sufficiently promising for America Online founder Steve Case to invest $500 million in a firm that purchases stakes in smaller firms that set up the clinics, Revolution Health Group. These clinics appear to be convenient and cost saving, hence would likely mushroom before our very eyes, but what does this portend for the insurance industry? Based on a simple business model, essentially a medical clinic that outside company operates, with staff mostly nurses and/ or physician assistants, these clinics provide a limited range of rudimentary tests and treatments at a lower cost than a doctor s office. Would this phenomenon, which incidentally has a different origin in the UK, where it is part of a deliberate government effort to move health services into the community, spread to Canada and other countries? These in-store clinics, for examples Quick Care at the Omaha Hy-Vee; Revolution s RediClinic, and MinuteClinic, which has 70 clinics in CVS pharmacies, Target Stores and Cub Foods supermarkets, are different from the so-called doc in a box stand-alone clinics, also increasingly common in the US. With patients requiring no appointments and open after regular business hours, many believe that these clinics provide ready access to care and could be the only healthcare service portal in certain places where GPs are few or lacking, besides offering the convenience of seeking help for a troublesome cough while in the grocery, shopping. Another significant aspect of this phenomenon is that these clinics list the price of care on a message board, giving patients the opportunity to shop around for care, which would overall make treatments in these clinics, which run minimal overheads, competitive and affordable. Some of them accept insurance plans, and charge only the co-payments but others will not accept co payments but will their clients a detailed receipt for submission to insurance providers. Some criticize these clinics for disrupting the continuity of care, but the phenomenon provides another instance of the changing healthcare landscape, how it affects the health insurance industry, and the role that healthcare ICT could play in solving the problem of continuity of care that id of concern to its critics. It also highlights how market forces could also be forces of innovation and creativity. In this regard, one could expect this business model to grow, and become even more sophisticated, and with Wal-Mart for example, having thousands, of outlets all over North America, including Canada, what implications would such developments have not just for health insurers, but for government s efforts at human resource developments in both the medical and paramedical fields. Could this be an interim solution to the acute shortage of medical personnel in some countries, and in underserved areas of others? Would there be need for government to regulate practice in these clinics, and indeed, prices of care? Are there issues of certification involved? What are the prospects of even one malpractice suit literally putting an abrupt end to this phenomenon? The answers to these questions would likely be important concerning the future of this emergent health service model. Developments in medical research are also going to continue to influence health insurance as the following examples show. Insurers might have known for sometime that women with heart attacks do not have the same symptoms as men with the same condition do, but would results from the massive Women's Ischemia Syndrome Evaluation (WISE), which have at last provided evidence to explain why, have any effect on insurance policies for men vis-à-vis women? How would the fact according to WISE investigators that doctors are missing the diagnosis in up to three million women with coronary heart disease because of the differences in their clinical presentation compared to men influence insurers' risk evaluation? The results of the WISE studies, published in the supplement to the February 07 2006 issue of the Journal of the American College of Cardiology, explained that in women, plaque, the fatty substance that clogs arteries in individuals with atherosclerosis, spreads out widely throughout the vessels rather than as in men, accumulating in specific locations. This explains why some women whose angiograms, results of imaging exam to identify partial or total occlusion of coronary arteries, are normal, may be at high risk for ischemic heart disease or heart attacks. Women also tend to have a different and more severe form of vascular disease than men. They also tend to have blockages in the tiny feeder vessels in the heart and to have stiffer, more inefficient aortas, defects that also usually do not show in angiograms, overall reducing women's chances of receiving aggressive treatments, for example using tiny flexible tubes, termed stents to open up arteries. Because the chances of being undiagnosed and untreated are therefore high in women, they are at higher risks of their condition progressing to major heart attacks. Indeed, about 50% of American women do not know that heart disease is the number one cause of death among women, but studies such as WISE is likely to change this under-recognition of the risks that they face with heart disease. Should the fact that also in the US, more than 250,000 women each year die from ischemic heart disease or related conditions, this number expected to rise with the graying of the population concern the insurance industry? Would the increasing awareness of these risks by women increase the numbers of them signing up for health insurance? Harvard researchers reported in the February 01, 2006 issue of Circulation: Journal of the American Heart Association, that cardiovascular disease causes 1 in 2.6 deaths in women and according to the US Centers for Disease Control and Prevention (CDC,) 38% of deaths in women compared to 22% for all cancers. Should the health and insurance industries, and other healthcare stakeholders not become more aggressive in health education campaigns alerting women to these risks? What role could healthcare ICT play in effectively getting the word out? Also in Circulation, Harvard researchers reported that obesity is a significantly greater risk factor for heart attacks than a sedentary life style in women. Furthermore, studies also showed that increasing exercises without losing weight does not significantly reduce the risk, but that both do, and is the best way to reduce the risk. Regarding exercise, University of Texas researchers reported recently that a half hour exercise could improve mood in men and women suffering from clinical depression, and is a useful adjunct to conventional therapy for the condition, and British researchers concluded in a recent report that spontaneity often works when quitting smoking. What would insurers make of a recent research study in Taiwan published in the January 31, 2006 issue of the Canadian Medical Association Journal that showed that tallness is not always advantageous, at least for individuals suffering form diabetes? The researchers showed that tallness is an independent predictor of lower extremity amputation in such persons, which means that they should have closer monitoring for peripheral sensory loss and leg ulcer. Do these research findings not indicate influence that developments in healthcare, particularly advances in medical knowledge could have on the operations of this insurance industry? Furthermore, do they not highlight the interdependence of the trio of technology, health, and insurance in contemporary health affairs? In particular, these examples, underscore the need for health insurance firms to be cognizant of recent medical findings, which could make a significant difference to their evaluation of actuarial risks and pricing policies. It could also help them determine the areas that they need to focus on in future value propositions. Health insurers could offer their clients wellness programs for example tailored to specific age groups, gender, or disease category, as part of their value-added services. Incidentally, according to CDC, the prevalence of obstructive coronary artery disease is relatively low among premenopausal women, and women generally do not catch up to men in rates of coronary artery disease until they are in their 70s. Doe this mean that women should ignore the risks mentioned earlier? Certainly not, because in the first place, they could have a heart disease well before the seventies, and considering the risks of missed diagnosis, could be in grave danger without treatment of the condition. Indeed, both women and men should recognize the fact that the best way to prevent heart disease, is via exercise and weight loss. No one should wait until the seventies to take this advice to heart, and act on it. With new technologies developed at what some would consider a frenetic pace, opportunities abound, made possible by healthcare ICT to exercise and trim down suited to individual needs and abilities. For example, an elderly person of seventy might not be able to tolerate the physical demands of an exercise regime that a younger person would not find little tasking. Individuals also require different exercise levels based on their health condition, for example, if they have an underlying, even if non-cardiac, disease. Healthcare technologies would help address these peculiar circumstances successfully. The delivery of qualitative healthcare in our times has become imperative. Nonetheless, this must be within certain constraints, chief of which is budgetary. Again, the implementation of the appropriate healthcare ICT would facilitate the achievement of these goals. Because of their close ties with health insurance, the there is no disputing the link between the survival of any of them to that of the trio.

Saskatoon, February 3, 2006.

References

1. Interrelationships of poverty and disease. In. Winslow C-EA. *The cost of sickness and the price of health.* Geneva: World Health Organization; 1951. WHO Monograph Series, No. 7, Chapter 4.

2. Bell, C Devarajan S, Gersbach, H. *The long-run economics of AIDS: theory and an application to South Africa.* Washington (DC): The World Bank; 2003. Policy Research Working Paper 3128.

3. Sen, A. Health in Development. Bull World Health Organ 1999; 77: 619-23

4. Available at:
http://www.usatoday.com/printedition/news/20060203/a_medicare03.art.htm
Accessed on January 03, 2006

Copyright Bankix Systems Ltd. 2006

www.ingramcontent.com/pod-product-compliance
Lightning Source LLC
Chambersburg PA
CBHW031240050326
40690CB00007B/882